The Bloke's Guide
To Pregnancy

The Bloke's Guide To Pregnancy

Jon Smith

BALKON
media

First published by Hay House April 2004

This edition published by Balkon Media March 2021

Cover design: Balkon Media
Interior illustrations by e-Digital

To Alia, Ronin, Sonya & Aoife — May you each achieve all that you desire.

Contents

Message For The Ladies

If he is a first-time father, one thing you can be sure of is that your husband, boyfriend, partner, brother, uncle, friend, or whoever else you had in mind when you picked up this book, has no idea quite what he has just got himself into. I mean no idea at all! He's probably frightened and anxious, somewhat nonchalant and cold, happy yet sad, and most importantly, he has no one to turn to. Not his mates, not you, and certainly not his mum (for once!)

Pregnancy, it is well documented, is a magical journey, but there are numerous things that need to be answered, explained or illustrated, before the man who will receive this book can feel in control enough to enjoy the experience.

It's not that he's deliberately being obtuse about the pregnancy, or that he is putting up a wall of denial – at least not consciously. It's just our natural male reaction to anything we don't understand. Men need manuals. A + B = C. The ankle is connected to the leg, which is connected to the hip – straightforward, to the point, and honest. *The Bloke's Guide To Pregnancy* – no flowery prose or idealistic diatribe, no mutton dressed as lamb. We want it raw and unabridged: tell us how it is: what's the worst that can happen? What's the best that can happen? If the engine is smoking, what should we look at first – the air pressure or the oil?

Yes, he might occasionally look at one of the numerous books written about pregnancy for women, (one of the five or so that you have already bought?) to read up on the deep science and follow the progress of his unborn child on a week-by-week basis; but, to be quite frank, they can be a bit boring for us blokes and too detailed. We want the truth, in bite-size pieces as easy to digest as a packet of biscuits. This book tackles what is going on inside his head, not what *should* be going on. It is based partly on humble first-hand experience, partly on the product of over one hundred interviews with blokes who have lived to tell the tale – a few of whom even admitted to enjoying the experience. Whoever the recipient of this book is, let us take his hand (metaphorically, of course) and help him on his way. He might even say thank you, and better yet, arrive in time for the birth.

Message For The Blokes

The Bloke's Guide To Pregnancy is for any man whose partner is expecting a baby. Whilst there already exists a wealth of literature available on pregnancy, some of which may well be filling up gaps on your bookshelf already, most of it is quite rightly geared towards the woman, and men often find these books to be too technical, or generally unsuitable, or even sometimes quite derogatory about men and their role.

If you are keen to understand the changes that will occur in you and your partner over the next few months, then this book is for you. If you are keen to play as much of a role in your partner's pregnancy as possible, then this book is for you. If your partner handed you this book, in an attempt to answer some of the questions that you keep asking her, then this book is also for you.

Bloke-To-Bloke – Telling It How It Is

I began writing this book as a form of catharsis, soon after my partner, Lisa, miscarried for the third time in less than a year. I felt naive, ill-informed, and generally a bit lost. To my knowledge, there was little or no literature available for men regarding miscarriage, or any of the other unfortunate things that can happen during a pregnancy; and thinking back, there was little information regarding pregnancy in general, written specifically for, and by, a man.

Alia, our daughter, was born on 22 November 2000. During Lisa's pregnancy, I browsed through a couple of chapters from her pregnancy books. Although I've always been an avid reader, something about the tone of those books was alien to me, and I got the distinct impression that I wasn't the intended audience. Although there must have been about ten pregnancy books in the house, and occasionally as many more titles appearing, following visits to the library, I preferred Lisa to sift through the information and tell me the important bits.

What I needed was a book aimed at blokes. This wasn't available during Lisa's pregnancy with Alia, but for the many men now about to embark on the trip of a life- time that is your partner's pregnancy, hopefully this book will fill the gap.

Your partner becoming pregnant involved two people. The rearing of your child will (hopefully) involve two people. There is every reason that your partner's pregnancy should involve the two of you, together. As the father-to-be, your visits to and from doctors and midwives will most probably be limited, especially if you work full time. If your friends are anything like mine, then any talk about the pregnancy will be minimal – it's not the sort of thing us men like to talk about, is it?

For the sake of practicality, this book assumes that your partner's pregnancy will be reasonably straight-forward, from conception through to birth, although there is a chapter later on in the book covering some of the potential problems that can occur during a pregnancy. As well as drawing on my own experience of fatherhood, it is the culmination of numerous interviews conducted over, (ironically), nine months. Although everyone's personal experiences will be unique, I hope that it will help answer some of the questions you have about the next nine months of your life.

Section One

1. He Shoots, He Scores!

it's positive

... Finding Out

It was early in the morning, on a cold February day, when Lisa came running into our bedroom brandishing an innocent-looking white stick.

'I'm pregnant! ****! The line's blue!'

Those were the words that struck fear into a grown man. Those were the words that turned Mr Complacent into Mr Really Afraid. Those were the words that changed my life, forever. Even though the pregnancy was planned, my initial reaction was not good. I freaked out, and despite the forced smiles and feigned positive response, inside I was a complete mess.

The decision to propagate the species had been made by both

of us, two months before, during a very romantic dirty weekend in Prague. Lisa and I had been an item since the previous September, and things had progressed at a remarkable pace by anyone's standards. Lisa proposed the idea of having a baby while we were together in a basement wine bar. I wanted to say yes immediately, but given how much we had been enjoying the Absinthe, I thought it wise, mature and terribly responsible, to ask for a few days 'thinking time'. To make a short story even shorter, suddenly, after about two months of 'we're trying for a baby,' we had one coming. In all honesty, it took me at least a good two weeks to accept the news, and more importantly, to begin to support my partner in the adventure of pregnancy. For those few weeks I was not much use to man nor beast. I'm ashamed to say that I accused Lisa of deliberately stealing and benefiting from my seed, so that she could leave me, impregnated. I even suggested termination and generally besieged her with any number of pathetic excuses as to why this pregnancy, with me, was probably not a very good idea. My mind was working overtime to invent ever more exotic reasons why we were doing the wrong thing – it was the wrong time regarding our careers; I was the wrong sort of person to be a father; we could never afford a baby, ever. What about our house, car, mortgage, pets, holidays, life? The list went on and on and boiled down, quite simply, to me being a selfish sod!

Lisa listened to and empathized with my ramblings with the candour and good grace of a saint. She made it clear that she was having the baby regardless, and it was up to me whether or not I wanted to be part of the experience. I am pleased to say that after further reflection and having witnessed Lisa's conviction and strength of character, I eventually saw sense. Finally realizing the importance of what was happening, I rallied to the side of my partner – to join her on what was to be the adventure of a lifetime.

The First Hurdle: Taking It On The Chin

I do not think that my case is unique. Many couples who have discussed having a baby are shocked when a pregnancy is actually confirmed. Some fathers interviewed mentioned that although the baby was planned, they had not envisaged things happening as fast as they did: 'We'll start trying for a baby, and maybe one might come along in six to twelve months. That'll give me time to get used to the idea. There's no way she will become pregnant straight away … ' How surprised they were when in a matter of a few weeks or months their 'wishes' had come true.

Mark, one father interviewed, reported that his girlfriend dropped her little bombshell while he was reversing his expensive new car around the corner. Once he'd recovered from his near-heart attack and narrowly avoided crashing the car, it was all he could do to stagger to the nearby pub for a stiff drink. Many terrible rows with his girlfriend ensued on the subject of timing and his precious new car, which no doubt masked real feelings of stress and fear about the pregnancy. However, he did also report feeling as if he'd just 'scored a century for England'. Ambivalence is a very natural thing in first-time parents and in 99.9 per cent of cases will totally disappear with the first glimpse of cute offspring, if not well before.

Reactions from other interviewees ranged from complete elation to intense disappointment and even anger – all of which abated to some extent over time. One interviewee reported that he replied, 'Oh, that's nice. Are we having brown or white rice with the stir fry?' He does note, however, that it was his fourth child.

Of course, there will be just as many couples who did not plan a baby but react to the news much better. The point is, whether the pregnancy is unplanned or planned, whether you as a couple are married or unmarried, does not matter. What matters is that once you definitely decide you are going to have the baby, the quicker both parties can accept that, the quicker the experience can be shared and enjoyed.

As you are reading this book, I assume you are already some way into the pregnancy. (I'd be very impressed with any blokes reading this before their partner is pregnant.) If you took the news on the chin, well done. If you are still in a state of shock, there are many others, including myself, who are or were, in an equal state of quasi-catatonia. It will pass.

Time For A Little Soul-Searching

To understand why we don't all jump up and down for joy at the wonderful news, we may need to explore what it is that got us to this position. Could it be that we didn't think the whole thing through as carefully as we should have? Are we blokes even capable of thinking things through carefully? In my case, coupled with the immense fear of not being a responsible enough adult, I was concerned from a selfish point of view – how would this baby affect my personal cash flow; my weekends; my nights out; my holidays; my lazy mornings in bed?

Most of us panic when the news of the pregnancy is announced. If you do feel that your world is collapsing around you, you really aren't the only one. Sadly, the one person you would ordinarily confide in – your partner – is unlikely to want to hear about your worries or sudden change of heart, and that's what is the hardest to bear. Who else is going to listen? Certainly not your mates and even your mum is probably not going to be consulted on this one. It's a scary time and trying to sort through the barrage of thoughts is very hard.

There are, as always, exceptions to all rules and a few dads interviewed actually argued convincingly that they were truly delighted with the news that their partner was pregnant, both for the first time and even more so when expecting a second and third baby.

Get Things Into Perspective

Sometimes other events can help you get a sense of what's really important in your life. Kevin, an actor, was on location in Poland with his wife in the early weeks of her first pregnancy. Like most couples they had a few doubts about their ability as parents, and associated worries about money, their lifestyle and so on. On a rare day off, they visited Auschwitz. Witnessing the appalling atrocities of the camps somehow put their fears and worries about what they could give a child very much into perspective. They were immediately positive about the pregnancy and didn't look back.

There is still an awful lot to be done in terms of supporting your partner between now and the birth. Knowledge is the key, and I hope that some of the things you need to know can be found within these pages.

It's Good To Talk

Although I came to terms with Lisa being pregnant within a matter of weeks – coming to terms with actual fatherhood was not so straightforward. It is most definitely not the same thing, an issue explored throughout this book.

As a couple you may well have discussed pregnancy, birth and child-rearing in depth, before the pregnancy. Now that it has happened, it is well worth revisiting – talking about anything from the 'when you are' perspective, is incredibly different from 'now you are'. It is much easier said than done, but the conversation should include your fears as much as your mutual excitement. It would be very strange indeed if you had no fears about your impending fatherhood, the pregnancy and the birth, no matter how calm and collected a person you are. Although it is often thought that we men are 'emotionally lacking', it would be a very callous man indeed who didn't think, at least once, 'Will everything be okay?'

Of course, complete empathy will be difficult. And stuffing a cushion under your shirt, however comical you may think that is, probably won't help. We're the wrong sex and of a different physiological make-up. We will not be subject to myriad concoctions of hormones being released into our bodies daily. We will not suddenly want to eat gherkins by the jarful. We are probably not going to be carrying around up to three or four extra stones in weight, all piled around our stomach. Our body shape is unlikely to change too drastically at all during the nine months of our partner's pregnancy – and we do not have to bear the pain of giving birth. There is no shortage of colourful descriptions of this particular experience. One father interviewed said his wife had described the experience as 'like shitting a watermelon'.

Yes, in many ways we should count our blessings. Unless you tell someone your partner is expecting, then there are no outward signs that this is indeed the case. We won't experience random strangers asking us when the baby's due, or feeling it perfectly within their rights to grab at the bump and give our tummy a rub. Basically, we have it easy.

You're Just A Bloke, After All

As mentioned, you are going to witness a whole raft of physical and psychological changes in your partner in the coming months. So how do you prepare yourself for something that you may never fully understand when there are so many unknown variables to contend with? Well, accepting for a start that you won't fully understand it all is a step in the right direction. By realizing your limitations, you are halfway there. I am not encouraging apathy, merely that you recognize boundaries that cannot be transcended. Once we acknowledge that we can only learn so much and understand so much, we are in a better position to help our partners and ourselves. Knowledge will be the key to supporting your partner as much as possible between now and the birth.

The main reason that you do not fully feel part of the process, no matter how much you try to immerse yourself in the pregnancy, is that you will not be all-consumed by it. Most men will continue to work full time throughout the pregnancy. The physical changes are happening to your partner, not you. I truly believe that blokes are simply not able to take it all in – no matter how much they want to. It's a bit like if our father was to say that he was suffering with a particularly acute bladder disorder. We would of course be sad and concerned, but unless we had suffered from the condition ourselves, we couldn't possibly begin to empathize with his pain, suffering and fears. We would lend our support where we could, but we would never really know what his experience was like. Similarly, our partner is now pregnant and we desperately want to do everything we can to assist. But can we really know what she is going through? Of course we can't. We can support her though, and we can do that even better if we accept from the outset that we will never fully understand her experience.

Pecks And Pregnancy?

For starters, you're probably wondering if you're leading the right lifestyle, right now, to maximize your effectiveness during the pregnancy and beyond. Well, you probably are – after all, you managed to spend enough time with your partner to make a baby, so you must be doing something right.

What is a good lifestyle, after all? We all know that we should at least be healthy and all the rest of it, but this is really brought home when it dawns on us that in six or so years, someone is going to outrun us in the park. Now there's a sobering thought. I made all sorts of promises to myself. The two biggest were to pack in the cigarettes and to get fitter. I failed miserably on both counts. Officially, I blame work and the associated commute, but unofficially I am inherently lazy and would choose not to get out of bed every morning, if I wasn't forced to by a call of nature, or, more accurately nowadays, the demands of a three-year-old daughter.

This pregnancy is an ideal time for you to make some serious changes to your lifestyle, if you are that way inclined. Bear in mind that so much is now forbidden to your partner, it would actually make it easier on her if you were to follow suit – or at least refrain from wolfing down before her salivating lips some of the finest sushi available, followed by unpasteurized cheese smothered in yoghurt, all resting on a bed of live mussels, and washed nicely down with a few highly alcoholic cocktails.

Feeling Like The Class Dunce

From the planning stage and right through pregnancy women just know what's going on, or at least that's the impression we get. It can make us feel under pressure to catch up. From puberty onwards they have an inherent understanding of natural cycles being attuned to their menstruation cycle. We, on the other hand, are forced to consult calendars, and that leads to confusion about the actual length of pregnancy. Why do the books insist on working out the due date from the first day of her last period, rather than conception? Surely you can't possibly be pregnant immediately after a period, for what seem to be obvious reasons?

'But I wasn't even in the country when you last had your period!'

Maybe it's to do with being more fatalistic than women, but I don't think that we men soak up information in the same way that our partners do. The facts and figures that we try to feed into our minds are quickly forgotten or ignored. A tactic that really helped one interviewee was to subscribe to www.babycentre.com, a weekly news bulletin from a UK-based website. The only hard knowledge you need is the baby's due date. (You should really ask your partner if you haven't already.) You then receive a very succinct and straightforward explanation of the progress of your unborn baby, without any unnecessary padding. The interviewee in question found this invaluable in that it quenched his need for information about the physical growth of the baby, without being too detailed. For the brownie-point-hunters amongst you, it also meant that he could ask the right questions each week, winning him untold gratitude from his partner for being so interested and on the ball!

Been There, Done That

If this is your second or third experience of fatherhood, and you are reading this, then maybe you weren't paying as much attention as you should have, first time round! For most second- or third-time-around fathers the entire phenomenon of pregnancy, labour and birth has lost some of its zing. Both partners are much more pragmatic in their approach, which is understandable given the amount of time and effort a toddler or young child demands of you. 'Proven' fathers are, of course, just as ecstatic as first- timers at the prospect of being dads again; many even more so now they know what they've been missing, as one dad put it. But it is nigh on impossible to become quite as excited and enthusiastic about the pregnancy the next time round.

Unfortunately, this can lead to arguments about whether dad is particularly bothered about the second baby. Of course you are, but feeling the bump kick; the provision of endless backrubs; *and* being told off for having slightly pongy feet can wear a bit thin second time around. Fatalistic father will still have his worries about getting too excited too early and this may be misconstrued as callous disinterest. This tends to be part of the general male mindset during all pregnancies and interestingly we do not get better with experience. The first pregnancy has given us a false sense of security that is difficult to shed – if you've changed one oil filter you've changed the lot.

Most importantly, second pregnancies and births are generally easier than the first. Experience counts for an awful lot in this game and while each pregnancy has unique facets, you and your partner are creatures of habit and therefore in the pole position of having seen it all before. Most reassuring, of course, is that if number one child was born after a long labour, number two will more than likely be out in a jiffy. Result.

Simon, an interviewee, got into many heated arguments with his partner while they were expecting number two. He assured his partner that he was delighted at the news and was looking forward to meeting someone new (the baby, not another girlfriend). But he had exactly the same worries as first time round – if anything, they were amplified now that he had seen his firstborn grow up and go to school. He understood, more than ever before, how profound the pregnancy actually was, and it was not until the second baby was born that he could truly relax and be excited about being a father once again.

Second Hurdle: Telling The Folks, Friends … And The World

You may expect your respective relations' reactions to the announcement of a new arrival in the family to be unreserved joy. Not necessarily!

Parents don't always take the news well. My own parents were hardly jumping up and down with joy at the prospect, until the news fully filtered through a few weeks later. Just as the first trimester (first three months of the pregnancy) for blokes is a journey into the realm of accepting fatherhood, for your parents it marks the end of a huge and familiar phase for them, and the beginning of another, especially if yours is their first grandchild. Accepting we are going to become parents can be child's play compared to our parents accepting they are going to become grandparents. Many soon-to-be grandparents will go into denial about the situation: 'I'm not ready to be a grandparent. I'm only 55. I'm just not ready yet!' Well sorry about that, but you haven't got a lot of choice in the matter! This rather selfish reaction can understandably be upsetting. Just at the very time you might seek solace and advice from your (experienced) parents, they are having as much trouble accepting the news as you are. Looks like you're on your own again.

Likewise, don't think that all of your friends will be jumping for joy either. It is about the time that you announce your pregnancy that you learn, for the first time, that Andrew and Suzanne have actually been trying for a baby for the last nine months without success. Equally unbeknown to you, Polly has been yearning for a child since she first hooked up with Simon two years ago, but he is not ready. Or, Mark and Angela actually experienced two miscarriages in the last twelve months, but hadn't wanted to mention it before now. You also have to remember that your news will affect those friends who are not currently in relationships or, worse, are in unhappy relationships. Everything might be going great for you and your partner, but no one likes having their face rubbed in the dirt.

This happened to Paul and Sarah when they convened a meeting of friends at the local pub to tell everyone their good news, face to face, at the same time. They thought they had arranged everything just right, but no. Sandra spectacularly spoiled the party by getting completely loaded and announcing that, in her opinion, Sarah was far too immature to become a mother. It then came out that she had been harbouring secret desires for Paul – and if he wanted, there was still time to ditch Paula and get together with her. I think not. So be prepared: someone, somewhere may decide to choose this particularly succinct time to bring the general mood down a notch. Suddenly your lovely news opens a Pandora's box of envy, rivalry, competition and status. Your 'friends' may actually be treating pregnancy and birth as the latest consumer fashion; and no one likes the smart arse who gets there first.

Changing Images

To a certain extent we are all guilty of placing people in boxes and labelling them, and this happens more and more as we get older and tend to see our friends less frequently. They will remember you from when your relationship with them first began. If you were the outgoing, sporty, loud, flirty, cheeky-chappie of your school that's how they will remember you – even if that was twenty years ago. Everyone has a fixed perception of you that does not age. So when you reveal that your partner is expecting a baby, they may be a little shocked. They may have you billed as far more immature, reckless and irresponsible than you actually are. They may even fear for the child; an attitude that can be difficult for all concerned. It's important to remember that even if you have up to now been as immature, reckless and irresponsible as they say, the act of father-hood may well be the making of you.

Another profound change to accept is that you becoming a father makes you and everyone around you realize that they are all getting that little bit older. Along with your parents coming to terms with becoming grand- parents, your friends may also have to realize that they, too, are entering a new stage – they now have friends with children! They will come round to the idea, eventually!

Then there are the siblings. Who will have the first grandchild? We find ourselves involved in a race against brothers and sisters that we have been signed up to run (unbeknown to the runners) since puberty. Whose baby will look great and whose will just look 'nice'. Which child will be clever? Which one the artist? Which one the black sheep? Is the family name going to be continued? Of course, this can get worse rather than better as the child is growing up, the race then being over who talks first, walks first, has the highest exam marks, passed their Grade Eight in piano and so forth. Brotherly and sisterly love? Not necessarily when it comes to talking about your kids.

So Who's Supporting Me??!

One of the most frustrating things for us blokes is how the gender divide ensures that your partner is supported, even if just superficially, by other women, from the moment you announce the pregnancy. This continues right through to birth and beyond. Women literally flock around a new-born baby as if he or she was the embodiment of perfection, or immortality itself (maybe he or she is?). Mums (both hers and yours) are great at rallying around a pregnant woman. Whether some of the advice is always welcome is a separate issue, but it is lovely to see so much solidarity. If there is any rivalry or animosity between the in-laws, then it is put to one side, for a new baby is the ultimate peacekeeper and pacifier. On the other hand, the only support you will receive, if you're lucky, is a few pints down the pub and a bag of cheese-and-onion crisps. Grandfathers are often a bit naff about it all: focusing on the negatives; quick jibes about sleepless nights and dirty nappies followed by criticisms about your job, salary, house and car. Ah, the joys of living in a capitalist society.

A very honest and forthright grandfather admitted that he had not been over the moon when his son told him he was going to be a grandparent but, instead, had felt guilty. The thought of his own son becoming a parent brought back regrets and fears hitherto lying dormant in a quiet part of his mind. He had been away on business throughout his son's early years. He simply did not want to see history repeating itself. Although this reaction was a little unfair on the expectant father, it appears that it is not uncommon and therefore could be something to look out for.

Looking For Role Models

We must bear in mind that, except in very rare circumstances, our fathers did not change nappies. They were not expected to, either by their partner or society – and they certainly didn't volunteer. They lived in different times, and attitudes to everything, including child-rearing, were very different. Whilst we all love our parents, some of us cannot help feeling some disappointment in our fathers for their lack of nurturing influence – even though we know it wasn't deliberate. Many of us grew up when spanking children was all the rage; corporal punishment still went on in schools, at teacher's discretion; and our grandparents still adhered to the 'children should be seen and not heard' mentality.

In fairness to dads the world over, there wasn't the proliferation of pop-psychology and self-help books around then that strain the shelves of bookstores today. A man's role was to earn and the woman's role to rear. Dads did the best that they could under the circumstances. But this lack of clear role models can cause anxiety in the expectant father – you may well worry about being distant from your children, both geographically due to work commitments and emotionally. We worry about not being there when we are needed. What if I am not successful? What if I end up in prison? I'm not the greatest human being; I'm not going to be a good dad. Will I be a disappointment to my children?

Irrational and daft fears – we all have some. The good news is that children couldn't care less about your status, car, house or bank balance (unless they're wise enough to understand the word inheritance from very early on). They just want love, care, and your time.

In a matter of months your baby will be born. You will make mistakes, but remember there are no rulebooks. Child-rearing is an ongoing process – you're not trying to create a master race and your children are not clones of you. Malcolm put it this way: 'If you can't do something at work you would either hire somebody in, or you would train yourself up in that aspect. It should be same with your child – you read up on the subject, learn and try to do your best. Nobody can ask more than that.'

With A Little Help From My Friends?

Sorry to be brutal, but your friends will probably not be much use at all. Hers will be fantastic, full of advice and encouragement, whether they have children or not. Your friends with children will probably be too busy, too tired or too bored with the whole subject to even crack a joke about it. Talk to any other bloke about your concerns regarding the pregnancy and the subject will be changed, as soon as possible, to something far less esoteric, like the barmaid's backside or how Frank still owes a tenner from six months ago. Not wanting to be seen as a bit of a wet-blanket-worrier type, we go with the general consensus, keep quiet about what we really want to talk about, and before long even catch a glance of said barmaid's backside and nod in agreement.

That's where the guidebooks come into play, although you're not going to be seen dead looking at one on a busy tube journey across London, or any other city for that matter
... are you?

Everyone's Got The Bug – Or How The Whole World Changes Too

I suppose that if anything is playing on your mind, you will tend, even if subconsciously, to be looking out for examples of or references to it. However, nothing prepared me for quite how many pregnant women and small children in prams I suddenly saw on the streets once Lisa was pregnant. Had I been blind to all this before or had it just not registered? From the moment that Lisa made her announcement I started noticing nappy adverts for the first time. The number of people with 'Baby on Board' stickers in their car and the number of children sat in shopping trolleys staggered me. For years, driving to a shopping centre or retail park had usually resulted in me purchasing some books, clothes, or something for the computer. Now for the first time I was buying things from enormous retailers that sold baby-related products and toys. Although I had no prior need to know where these shops were, I equally had little need for a jewellers, but I could probably have given you directions to find one. Mothercare and Early Learning Centre? Well, I know where they are now. And I spent a small fortune at both.

The crossover between your old life and the new baby-related one can feel quite surreal at times. Tony, a high-flying city lawyer, found it particularly bizarre to be having an intricate discussion about an important contract deal, by mobile phone, whilst waiting in the buggy queue at Mothercare World in Basingstoke.

'I'll see you in court!'

'Excuse me?'

'Not you! Sorry. Err. I'm after a highchair, suitable from birth?'

If Looks Could Kill

A strange thing happens to members of the public when they see that your partner is pregnant, especially during the latter months of her pregnancy. I still treasure the memories I have of both men and women assessing Lisa's bulge and revealing, quite unintentionally, their true thoughts of pregnancy and how it would affect them. Although there were exceptions, most men aged between eighteen and thirty would pull a face of abject horror, as if they were mentally saying to themselves, 'I must avoid that at all costs'. A quickening of their step, and they were gone – childless and very, very relieved about the fact. Women of a similar age reacted in one of two ways: abject horror, much like their male counterparts, or a small smirk, which I can only assume was a tiny bit of empathy and even, 'What if?'

The humour for me was when a couple would pass, assess the bump, and then the man would avoid eye contact with Lisa and pretty much everything other than the pavement, while the woman would smile.

Then there is the spotting of another expectant couple. Maybe I'm wrong but there seemed to me some competitive natures at play with regard to who was closer to being a 'fully paid-up club member' and who had a whole lot longer to go. I think deep down I was trying to ascertain, in a fleeting glimpse, whether I was coping and 'looking the part' as well as the bloke walking towards me. I think Lisa was comparing maternity wear and wondering where on earth her opposite number had got that top. It is reassuring to see other couples in a similar situation, and although I wouldn't go so far as to suggest you should seek out other expectant couples, if you do happen to meet them, it can lead to a lasting friendship long after your respective children are born.

Finally, there are the couples with the new-borns in pushchairs or strapped on to a parent. Without fail they would glance at Lisa and both reveal a knowing grin. I must say that I, and probably Lisa too, would inadvertently pay more attention to the baby than the parents, wondering desperately what our unborn child looked like, and usually making a mental note not to buy our child a themed Babygro with floppy ears or antlers. (I deny, despite the photographic proof, that I bought Alia a Santa Suit for her first Christmas.)

The 3rd Hurdle: Your Changing Relationship

It is a sad irony that the one thing that should bring you and your partner even closer together is often the cause of relationships coming apart. But there is so much you can do to prevent this. For a start, if you and/or, your partner works full time, you can have your evenings together. You will doubtless have prior commitments, but nothing will be as important as this new life, busily growing in the womb. Your social life must and will alter during pregnancy, not just after the birth. Make what changes you can to your calendar immediately. If you are a couple that spends a lot of time together, make sure that this continues. If you are seldom home, begin to alter this habit now. Your presence at home is as important during the early months as it is towards the end.

Equally, it's important to maintain any recreational activities, especially sporting pursuits, that you normally indulge in; unless having a larger belly helps you empathize with your partner more ... The pregnancy should not mean that you cease all contact with friends, but what you could do is 'triage' events for their importance. This means weighing up the importance of said event, how much it means to you, and whether you could probably do without going.

One father I spoke to would take the cash he would have spent on a night out, place it in a pot, and then at the weekend buy a product needed for the baby – he argued that if he had just left the money in his account it would have been spent on something else, but by making the conscious decision to withdraw the funds he had something tangible and useful at the end of the week –

plus one less hangover!

Being with your partner for every waking moment is obviously not healthy. Encourage your partner to socialize as much, and for as long, as she is able. Continue to lead individual lives, but be more aware that she will probably welcome any increase in your presence. A common misunderstanding is that your role really kicks in when your partner is bulging with child and about to give birth; wrong. Your role starts the moment your partner tells you she is pregnant. It is during the first three months that your partner is at most risk of miscarriage. It is in the first three months that she will be coming to terms with the monumental changes in her body, and the unknown quantities of labour, birth and parenthood. And it is only in the first three months that you will be able to do pretty much everything you both did before the pregnancy. Enjoy and savour those early days together as much as possible.

While being supportive in pregnancy is not just about winning 'brownie points', simple acts will be noticed. Furthermore, if your partner is able to feel calm, appreciated and cared for, her blood pressure is more likely to remain within a safe limit, which will have a positive effect on the pregnancy, your partner's and baby's health, and possibly even the temperament of your unborn child.

There Is Life Beyond The Baby

If finances permit, and before the latter stages of your partner's pregnancy, when simply getting off the sofa will be a chore, make as much of an effort to go out as a couple as you can. If one or both of you are working full time, then it might be one of very few moments you get to speak to each other during the week. Use the evening to catch up and talk about the pregnancy, but also make sure you discuss other topics too. Your partner's pregnancy can become an all-encompassing experience for the two of you, but it's good to make sure any other interests are given room to grow too. If you are both film buffs, choose the cinema, until sitting in the chairs becomes restrictive and uncomfortable – but look carefully at what's on the bill. A tearjerker may not be the best idea, although you might not have much choice in the matter – there will probably be tears anyway, and lots of them.

It might also be a good time to get used to entertaining at home, if this is not something that you would ordinarily do. As the pregnancy progresses, your partner's ability to stay up late will vanish. On home turf this is less of an issue, and the comfort of familiar surroundings and the knowledge that her bed is only paces away can, in fact, have the effect of allowing her to stay up a bit longer.

Take A Break ... Together

Again, if finances permit, take a holiday or a short break during these early months. Even if you are only able to muster a night or two in a bed and breakfast in a neighbouring city, the two of you will enjoy it. Likewise, if you can swan off to the Maldives for two weeks, I'm more than sure you will enjoy that too! It's simply another way to spend more 'quality' time with each other. Whether you decide to change the venue from your home to a hotel in this country or overseas, it does not matter. For the first few months of your child's life, you will be unlikely to have the option, or the inclination, to go away. Catch the opportunity while you can. You'll both appreciate the time and intimacy. If you decide to go on car journeys, be prepared for lots of puke stops in the early months and lots of wee stops in the later months. Between you and me you might want to surreptitiously invest in some plastic bags and some air freshener and keep them handy in the car...

The Fourth Hurdle: What's It Gonna Be?!

There are those who do and those who do not want to know the sex of their child before birth. Currently in the UK, each NHS authority can decide whether their policy is to allow parents to know, or whether the gender should remain unknown. At Hemel Hempstead hospital, for example, we could ask to be told the baby's gender. Some friends of ours, in Reading, could not – although they later paid for a private scan to find out. The decision to discover your baby's gender is your own. For some couples it makes a big difference to them, especially if they are expecting a second or third baby. If you do find out, it allows you to be more specific when choosing names and toys and clothes – although most items are pretty much unisex, especially for the first three months.

As a baby's gender can be incredibly important to some parents, I suppose that the issue of knowing can become a problem if one partner wants to and the other doesn't. I am sure that there are ways round it. The nurse, for example, could pass the partner who 'wants' a folded piece of paper after the scan. It is probably easier for all concerned, however, if you both agree either to know or not. This could be one of many compromises that you or your partner will make during her pregnancy. Also, bear in mind that the scans to determine gender are not always 100 per cent accurate and it is not unheard-of for the hospital to get it wrong. Keith, when interviewed, recalled a story he had heard about a couple, although he wasn't sure whether it was myth or reality. With both initially undecided about finding out their baby's gender, in the end, the mother decided to find out, and kept the knowledge from her partner. All was well until a month or so before the birth, when presents started arriving from her parents. There was definitely a girl theme to all the gifts, and after a chance remark from his mother-in-law the soon-to-be-dad realized that he was actually the last to know!

Sons and Daughters, Love and Laughter … And Happiness

Gender preference is potentially life threatening! You might think that a little exaggerated, perhaps, but I would advise that if you do have a strong preference, and it isn't for a girl, keep very, very quiet. If there is a single conclusion that can be drawn from the interviewee answers, it is that 112 out of 117 men wanted a boy and the vast majority of their partners were hoping for a girl. Most had kept quiet about their choice, (possibly sensing inherently that this was wise, like knowing not to put your hand in a furnace or not to jump off a large building). The few that spoke up, generally received a furious response.

I wouldn't change Alia for the world, but looking back to when Lisa was expecting, although the mouth said one thing, the heart said something else. I wanted a boy who would be great at football. He would be strong, wise, courteous and noble; in touch with his emotions but very much a man's man; confident and dynamic, brave and fair: a 'Mini-Me', able to pick up where his Dad (thinks he) left off. I felt I would instinctively know what to do with a boy; what they might like to play with, how to talk to them, take them for their first pint, and so on. I had it all mapped out in my mind; everything would be okay. When we were choosing names, I took my time over boys' names, finding the process difficult; we managed only two in nine months. Choosing girls was easy, as I assumed we weren't going to have a girl, and thus we created a list twenty strong.

One father, when asked if he would prefer a boy or a girl, repeatedly answered that he wasn't fussed. Again, the question was asked and again came the same response. Two months before the birth he was asked for the umpteenth time. He wrote down the exchange to the best of his recollection:

'What do you really want? When you picture yourself, a year from now, are you holding a baby boy or a girl?'

'I dunno, put like that I suppose I can see a boy.'

'I knew it! What's wrong with girls? I'm a girl and you liked me enough to get me into this state? What are you afraid of, Graham? Worried what your Mum might say, or your mates? I suppose you think that having a girl is some sort of booby prize. Well, I hope it is a girl just to spite you, you inconsiderate arse!'

The findings are conclusive; whatever you want, say you don't mind either way.

Mark was one of two boys and his father had always longed for a girl. All throughout his girlfriend's pregnancy they both had to endure endless remarks from his dad along the lines of 'Not that I mind, but it would be lovely to have a little granddaughter.' When a son was duly delivered, Mark called his dad from the hospital brimming with news of the family's first grandchild. There was a disappointed pause, and then a grudging, 'Oh well, that's alright then.' Nearly two years later, every time the now doting grandad remarks on his 'smashing grandson' he is mercilessly reminded of this.

Better The Devil You Know?

Many interviewees who were hoping for a boy were experiencing what could be called fear of the unknown. We are men, and we like to think we know what makes us tick. Women, however, are different – some even argue that they come from a different planet. To bring a boy into the world would simply be easier. We would know what they liked and disliked, almost without having to ask. Girls are strange creatures, so delicate and petite. Would I hurt her with rough play? What if I hold her hand too tightly or I cuddle her too hard? What if I were to lose my temper and shout; would the poor girl live her life in absolute dread of her father?

I had a particular fear of bathing babies, especially girls. I would at some stage I realize, have to clean her bits and I so did not want to do that. It certainly wasn't a fear of poo or wee it boiled down to a fear of viewing my child in a sexual way – something that repulses all rational men. Our fears intensify when further we start to think of our daughters becoming teenagers. How will we react when she announces she has a boyfriend? Or she's pregnant? Or living with someone? Having spent so many of our formative years chasing after women, with only one or two goals in mind, we realize that there will be younger versions of ourselves prowling the classrooms, the bars and the clubs, and we don't want to expose our daughters to reality. Of course this argument is flawed, given that if we have a boy we will be positively encouraging him to find girlfriends as soon as he is able. Ah, the joy of double standards. For the interviewees who had had or were expecting their second or third child, the desire for a boy or girl was directly affected by the hand that nature had dealt them already. Most fathers wished for a balance of gender, but none said that they were desperate for a boy or a girl, just that they would prefer one or the other. This might have had something to do with their partners being present at the time of the interview …

Ironically, although us blokes think we're going for the easier option if we are presented with a choice, we have it all wrong when it comes to wanting a boy. Little boys often are, not to put too fine a point on it, complete psychos. They will destroy your prized possessions, and grin while they do it. They have extremely bad tantrums and will hit both you and your partner very hard in the face … a lot. And, as they get older, they only become worse. In fact, they will become as obnoxious as you were at the same age – and that wasn't a pretty sight!

Girls, on the other hand, are of course both beautiful to look at and in their demeanour. They are often courteous and graceful, and although your prized possessions might get scratched and damaged, it won't be with the same malicious intent. More importantly, when you're fat, old and bald, your daughter will still love you (at least enough to visit once a year). But maybe I'm biased on the matter.

How About Maximus?

Choosing the name of your child is an absolutely massive responsibility. Your child will be left with the consequences of your decision for the rest of his or her life. It is something that often occupies parents-to-be throughout the whole of the nine months pregnancy, and none of the fathers interviewed said that he managed to choose a name without at least one or two arguments with his partner. We all have names that mean a lot to us and names that we cannot stand, and you are probably living with someone who thinks in exactly the opposite way than you do. No matter how much you might like Obadiah, your partner will hate it. She will suggest another name, and you will hate it just as much. This form of name tennis can go on for weeks.

We all tend to want to avoid the most popular names or those that are particularly fashionable at a given time, usually the name of a celebrity or more commonly a celebrity's child. But equally we have to bear in mind the accessibility of a name; will her friends and teachers be able to spell it without having to ask every time. Will she be fed up, by the age of five, of saying, 'That's with a C, not a K?' Likewise, there is nothing worse than having the same name as ten other people in a class – all things to bear in mind when you are choosing.

Do not be alarmed if you have not chosen by the time your baby is born. Some parents swear that they cannot commit to a name until they have seen the baby; others completely change their mind a few days after the birth (before the baby's birth is registered). There are numerous books and websites available that will list everything from the popular to the extreme; be sure to keep a list somewhere of what you considered – it will make superb reading in about eighteen years: especially for Adam, who narrowly escaped being called Jeremiah; Alexander, whose father was for some time insisting on Deepak, while mother favoured Merlin (apologies to all Jeremiahs, Deepaks and Merlins); and yours truly, who escaped being Shamus Hamish Smith by a very narrow margin. Have fun, but be fair!

2. 'Let's Talk About Money, Money'

Me, Hunter-Gatherer!

Regardless of whether you happen to be earning more than your partner or not, most men like to feel that they provide the hunter-gatherer function in the family unit. Obviously we don't go out clubbing the nearest mammoth on the head any more; but something inherent, whether it's just natural or a product of social conditioning, brings this feeling to the fore of our mind the moment we learn that our partner is expecting a baby. We need to provide financially for our family and only the lucky few will not worry about their finances at some point during, if not entirely throughout, the pregnancy. Becoming a father means, for most of us, having actually to be sensible and careful with our money, possibly for the first time ever in our lives. If we have problems with debt or money management these can seem overpowering and can be one of the most common reasons why many men cannot enjoy the pregnancy as much as they are expected to.

Plan Your Poverty!

It can't be stressed enough that becoming a father will bring your average monthly spend up considerably. Unless you are particularly well off, any addition to your family is going to have an effect on your finances. The cost of a child is very real, and it starts long before your baby enters the world. Your wallet will be stretched as much as your emotions, the estimated cost of a child from birth to eighteen being valued at around £70,000-£100,000 in the UK, and $100,000 - $140,000 in the US. Apart from anything else, if you have both been working, you will be trying to cope with one less salary coming in at the same time as having all these additional costs to cover. Many of the fathers interviewed stated that, prior to the pregnancy, both they and their partners were taking home salaries and sharing costs. For at least the length of maternity leave, they now had the additional cost of another member of the family plus the loss of one of the salaries (and in many cases the father's partner was earning the greater salary). And in the cases where these partners gave up work completely, this obviously put even more pressure on the man of the house.

Even if she does intend to go back to work, no matter what help your partner may receive from the state or her employer, unless it matches her income pound for pound (or dollar for dollar), you are going to be living on reduced means. And that extra cash for all those baby essentials has to come from somewhere. Yes, there is always the option of robbing a bank, but the chances of being caught are tremendously high, and you are not going to be an effective parent whilst sitting in a box in Wandsworth, or San Quentin. The more responsible (no need to look so smug) among you will have begun amassing savings from the moment you learnt that your partner was pregnant. Alternatively, you may both have savings already and that 'rainy day' you were saving for may just turn out to be a hungry, naked baby.

Get Organized Now

Most of us are guilty at some stage of running a bit riot with the various forms of credit so easily available from the most unlikely of places. (You go in for some fresh broccoli and come out with a loan from your supermarket!) I was no exception. Student loans, bank loans, credit cards and a severe lack of savings all added up to making my personal balance sheet a dream for the lenders but pretty miserable for me. Although I maintained that I was generally unaffected by Lisa's pregnancy, something must have kicked in because suddenly I was looking at a consolidation loan, reduced monthly repayments and even a pension!

Take it from me, with a full-time job and a new-born baby you will not have the time, let alone the concentration span, to reorganize your finances after the birth. Financial planning and managing money is a science, and there are numerous books on the subject that will allow you to plan and cope successfully. Yes, it is an additional cost in the short term, but buying the books could save you thousands over the long term. It is extremely important honestly to assess your finances, as early on in the pregnancy as you can. It's a horribly complex and boring procedure but it must be done. As your baby begins to change and grow in the womb, so too will your thoughts about what should happen next – and how much it will all cost.

Debt Bustin'

Debts are the bane of most of our lives. If we don't have credit cards and loans then it's the overdraft that's costing us money every month of the year. There is an argument that the financial houses make borrowing and saving deliberately confusing and laborious so that you become trapped. If it took such an effort to set up the existing loan, do you really want to go through the process again with another? No, you might just continue to pay an astronomical interest fee every year and find that the principal loan hardly moves at all.

Yes, it is boring ploughing through the small print, but it's well worth the effort. For example, just lowering your interest rates by 1 per cent might see you saving hundreds, if not thousands of pounds a year, depending on the size of your debt. The simple rule is to pay off the debts that are incurring the highest rates of interest first; once these are clear concentrate on the next one down. This might mean planning for the next year or even the next ten years, (longer still if you are including a mortgage too). Sometimes the truth hurts, but better that it hurts and you are reacting to it, than continuing to spend as you did before the pregnancy, without making any allowances for your baby.

Tony and Michelle led a heady lifestyle before junior came along. Their years together were peppered with short city breaks all across Europe and they enjoyed it, a lot. The lifestyle continued throughout the pregnancy and into the early months of their baby's life – one of very few six- month-olds with a passport to make adults jealous. Then, unsurprisingly, it all came tumbling down. The lenders refused to give any more credit, the banks were calling in debts and there was no easy way out. This story ends with a very generous bail-out from their parents, but they were lucky.

Lighten Up!

On the flip side of this, I did meet a couple called Bill and Madeline who were doing very well for themselves in London. It would be fair to say that they were a little bit mean with their money. He was working as a chartered surveyor and she was a teacher. They had always regarded themselves as 'careful with money'; close pals would word it 'extremely careful with money, in a way that was embarrassing to their friends in social situations'. Once pregnant, Madeline decided not to continue with her profession, and although Bill's income was still great, they vowed to 'protect their cash flow', which seemed to mean 'leeching off their friends in an increasingly embarrassing way'.

The moral of the story is that although you do have to be more careful with cash, you must still enjoy yourselves when you can. Having children should not mean that you have to become ultra-conservative with money, but it does mean that you have to budget. Do go out as a family when your baby arrives, do have fun and do have the occasional lavish shopping spree – even if it is for the latest toy fad. Don't live like a hermit monk and equally don't become, or continue to be, extravagant. Find and maintain a happy medium.

If we look at everything too closely from a financial perspective, it is probably cheaper not to get out of bed in the morning! Life has to go on, and although you will never actually blame your child for costing so much, or look at them as the spoiler of your pre-pregnancy financial bliss (well, maybe very, very rarely), equally you must prepare for them.

Get Your Benefits Sorted

There is some (not a great deal, but some) help available if you are really struggling financially. It differs (in name) depending on your marital status, but there is tax relief for married and unmarried couples, once you have a baby. Once the baby is born, your partner will also receive Child Benefit if you are in the UK.

At the time of writing, thanks to recent UK legislation, all (female, obviously) employees are entitled to a minimum of 26 weeks' Ordinary Maternity Leave regardless of how long they have worked for an employer. Employees with 26 weeks' continuous employment, or more, are also entitled to a period of Additional Maternity Leave. This starts at the end of the Ordinary Maternity Leave period and lasts for a further 26 weeks. In essence, up to a year.

The new right to paid paternity leave for dads is in addition to the 13 unpaid weeks' parental leave entitlement. Unfortunately, the entitlement is only two weeks' paid leave and is at a rate of £100 per week (or 90 per cent of the employees average weekly earnings if this is less). Not a lot to get excited about, but a step in the right direction. Hopefully your contract or your partner's contract with your employers will have some additional benefits relating to maternity or paternity leave. Contact information for useful organizations relating to social security and benefits are listed in Chapter 12.

Get Hitched?

Well, if you're not already, and it doesn't cross your mind, it might well cross hers. More and more children are being born out of wedlock, which is something that I am all for. However, there is a real case for marriage once a baby is on the way, and although you might be happy to maintain the status quo it is common for your partner and your respective families at such a time to be keen to see a ring or two being worn in the near future. As far as your partner is concerned, she is understandably protecting her interests. If you are not married and she gives up her job to look after the baby, she is in a very vulnerable position should you break up. However, financial headaches of this kind will not be the best framework for a romantic celebration. Pressure from family to hear the wedding march can become tiresome and now is not really the right time to have any additional pressure put on you as a couple.

Weddings are stressful, expensive and time-consuming events (not unlike the pregnancy that you are now part of), and therefore it is a good idea to make any huge decisions about this as early on in the pregnancy as you can. Many mothers-to-be will want to postpone the marriage until a good few months after the birth; they may claim it's because it will be less stressful but really it's because they'll be able to fit into a much more glamorous dress.

At one level, marriage may cement your relationship, and since you are having a baby together it may feel like the right thing to do. Let's face it, having a child together is pretty much as close as you can get to another human being, so maybe marriage isn't all that bad an option. It is also important to remember that getting married may or may not become a big issue for your child later on in life. Whose surname will the child take? Is the surname question already causing arguments in the household? Marriage pretty much settles this. You will also have heard the argument that if you are going to get married eventually, why not now – certainly as far as presents are concerned it might be the ideal time to get some of the bigger items bought for you!

I would certainly treat the new baby as an important variable in the decision to get married, but it should not be the only reason. If you work well as an unmarried couple already, and maybe even have misgivings about the institution of marriage, then you might be as well to leave everything as it is. We did, but the resolve of even the most adamant of us breaks in time and when Alia turned three I did the honourable thing and made an honest woman of Lisa – I'm now quite into the whole marriage trip and even got a fine-looking ring out of the whole deal.

Wills

While we're on the subject of legal matters it is also of paramount importance that you and your partner make a will, if you haven't done so already. This is necessary if you are married but even more so if you are not. Wills are reasonably straightforward and not too expensive, at least not in comparison to the potential legal fees that either you or your partner may incur if you have to resort to litigation after a death.

All a will is really saying is that you want certain items of property or other investments to go to specific people when you die. Just as you control the distribution of your wealth (estate) when you are alive, these are your instructions after your death.

Dying without a will means that the state wins, and it will be a hard battle for your family to win back what should rightfully be theirs, without at least paying a penalty. I have listed some online resources in Chapter 12 that may be of assistance. Once your baby is born you should revisit the will to include him or her – assuming you would like your child to benefit!

You, Mummy!

Many women are adamant that they will return to work, full time, at the end of their maternity leave. Right up until the eleventh hour they are ready to do it, until push actually comes to shove (so to speak). Suddenly they decide that there is really no choice between trekking into work, enduring the stress and boredom and endless office politics, or walking around the park gurgling at their beautiful little baby. Seriously, childcare is not cheap and may even cost more than your mortgage or as much as one of your salaries – after all, whoever is doing the caring is doing it as their full-time job. And your partner may come to the conclusion that it simply isn't practical, either financially or logistically, for her to return to work straightaway.

Tony's wife Linda had a challenging but enjoyable job in advertising, which involved a long commute on the London Underground and lots of evening functions. Not a problem when she was young, free and single but once she was pregnant and started researching childcare and nurseries, she realized how impractical returning to work was going to be. Many nurseries financially penalize parents who pick their children up late; some even 'expel' them or report them to social services (!) if it happens too often. Apart from the physical toll of trekking halfway across London every day, in a perpetual state of anxiety about being late either for work or for the nursery, Linda simply wouldn't have been able to continue putting in the kind of hours she previously had. Tony also worked irregular hours, so couldn't help either. Much as she loved the job she had tenaciously worked so hard for, she had to acknowledge that her baby would have to come first. Poppy is now eighteen months old and Linda is freelancing from home; a compromise that means she doesn't earn as much, or experience any of the glamour and fun of her previous job, but one that works well for the family's current situation.

Understand and Support Her

Your partner will have to consider factors like these when making that all-important career/motherhood choice. If she has been working full time for any length of time, and loves her job and/or her independence, the question of whether and when she returns to work is going to be a very tough call for her to make. If she has been used to having her own money, she is going to have to adjust to being financially dependent on you for a while. Whatever she decides, be as understanding as you can and support her in her decision. Believe me, staying at home looking after a demanding six-month-old is not the easy option.

Whatever you decide, the shocking cost of either losing one salary or paying almost the equivalent of it for child- care is a massive financial actuality that needs to be organized and fully thought out, long before you need to implement your choice. Arrange as much as you can towards your child's care before the birth; it will be a huge weight off your mind once achieved. Phone around the local nurseries and get a quote for full- and part-time care, if this is a route that you are considering. Unfortunately, 'choosing' childcare is often little to do with choice and everything to do with money.

Silver Buggy-Walkers

It is no surprise that these days more and more grandparents are stepping into the breach, and looking after the baby. Enlisting a family member you trust completely and who is happy to help out is becoming the number-one option for many busy young couples. During the course of my interviews, I was amazed at the lengths that many grandparents will go to help out and be involved in their grandchildren's upbringing. Nick, a North Londoner, told me how his 65-year-old mother-in-law caught the train from Cornwall every Sunday afternoon – a journey of over five hours – to look after eight-month-old Charlie while his wife was at her part-time job, and caught it back again every Wednesday afternoon. His experience was not unusual – it seems there are whole networks of parents and grandparents regularly tracking up and down the country with nappy bags and babygros. This isn't going to be possible for many but it's certainly worth exploring creative ways to make childcare more affordable and enjoyable.

Oh! Suits You, Sir!

And then of course there's that new-fangled phenomenon, the house husband. I had four months of being Mr Mum and whilst it was a great bonding experience, and at times thoroughly enjoyable (certainly when compared to sitting in traffic on the M1) it was also, without a shadow of a doubt, the hardest job on the planet. Exhausting, overwhelming and sometimes infuriating go some of the way to describing the complexity of looking after a baby – and I only had four months of it!

But then I met Mark, a technical whiz with an enviable CV (and large house in a posh London suburb) who swapped it all for a little bundle of joy called Daniel. He left software development behind and never looked back. Mark took to the role of bringing up a baby as if it had always been his life calling. Undisturbed by being the only bloke at mother and toddlers' groups; happy to throw the occasional coffee morning himself; and a dab hand at creating exciting recipes with nothing more than a carrot and cauliflower – he was, and remains, in his element.

The point is it can be done. Yes, you might still get the odd funny look, but thankfully the stigma has gone and it is perfectly acceptable for dad to be mum when it comes to rearing children. Again, whatever your decision, remember that there is no right or wrong way to bring up children.

The Career v Fatherhood Conflict

If you're not planning such a drastic lifestyle change, will being a father hamper your career? Will your new baby mean that it is less likely you're able to hang around the office, or the pub, until seven or eight at night? And will the lack of your presence at said office or pub be held against you in the next round of promotions, which funnily enough are about the time that your partner will be giving birth? Is now a good time to ask for paternity leave?

Most of us, in our own way, are ambitious. It is very human to want to succeed or even excel at things. When it comes to our careers, we want to give ourselves some purpose, possibly even help others:

'No, really Madam, it's so much more than a cooker, you can't live without it.'

But primarily, we want to provide for our family and ourselves. Ironic then, that creating this family, or more accurately becoming a father, may hamper our career right at the time we need everything to be better. Or at least that's how we think it might affect us.

Right Job?

In fact, in a bizarre way becoming a father can actually be the best thing to happen to your career. Not going to the pub until eight, both during pregnancy and especially once the baby is born, will save you an absolute fortune, not to mention all the lost mornings spent nursing those hangovers. Of course you won't see any of the extra cash because it will be well spent on clothes, food and nappies for your baby; but think about it: where would the money for such items have come from otherwise? The money tree at the bottom of the garden, perhaps?

I, too, became acutely aware of our domestic situation and panicked horribly when Lisa said that she was pregnant. Was our house big enough for three? Of course it was. Was I in the right job? Well, financially, with both partners earning, yes; but I was aware that we would be losing one salary and suddenly all the bills would be paid for out of one little pot. Unfortunately, I jumped from the frying pan into the fire. I did find a role that meant more money, more benefits and status, but I wildly underestimated the effect of the commute. I resigned from one job which was just down the road (in relative terms) and that took me 45 minutes to get to and from each way, to take on a job over 100 miles away. In retrospect, not one of my better decisions. In fact, I only lasted for seven months before I gave it up in search of less wealth but something that meant I was actually home every night.

Martin, a deep-sea diver for an oil company, reflected on his somewhat dangerous occupation and decided to re-skill during his partner's pregnancy – he now works as a consultant to the same company, but with his feet firmly on dry land. Interestingly enough, he cited watching football as his main influence in making the decision – the form of a number of players he followed had significantly dropped once they became fathers –

Quite understandably, their mind was elsewhere. Whilst Martin had no doubts in his mind about his competence in his job, if he had 'lost form' 75 metres below the surface, it would have had far more dire consequences than missing a hat trick.

Mr Responsible

I used the 'excuse' of fatherhood to avoid the extra hours at work and to reassess what career I actually wanted to be working towards. It took the pregnancy to give me the confidence I needed to put my interests first, rather than the profits of a nameless, faceless corporation. Once I'd changed my job, for the first time in my working life I could leave the house at 8.00 and be back at 18.00 – for me that was bliss.

I thought that I was quite radical in giving up my job pretty much as soon as I found out we were having a baby and finding a better-paid one, despite the horrible commute it involved. But it appears that quite a few of you go through the same thought process and end up doing something similar. Many interviewees used the news of the pregnancy as a bargaining chip with their employers, often with magnificent results. It has certainly got to be worth a try if it might result in a better salary, or perks, or even more favourable hours.

In fact, many of my interviewees said telling their bosses of their impending fatherhood was actually a surprisingly positive experience. They felt they were immediately given more respect, as if they had miraculously gained more gravitas and graduated from immature lad to mature man-of-the-world. Bosses who were proud fathers themselves were especially full of bonhomie, suddenly bringing out photos of gangling offspring and sharing all manner of avuncular advice, not all of it welcome. All in all, it typically proved to be a bonding experience. Alas, the situation is still often the complete opposite in the world of the working woman.

For all my holier-than-thou advice in these early chapters, I was away a lot on business during Lisa's pregnancy and that is time I will never be able to recoup. Although I regret it, I am pleased to say that I saw sense before Alia's birth and managed to get the timing right between resigning from one job and starting the next, which gave me an enviable six weeks (unpaid – you can't have everything!) at home with Lisa and Alia during the critical early days.

Home, Sweet Home?

Of course, everyone's living situation is unique. However, for the purpose of this book I have assumed that both partners are living permanently under the same roof. Apologies if you are reading this while sitting on a rig in the North Sea, or overseas in the Forces.

The place you choose to live in is likely to be the biggest financial investment you will ever make. This becomes even more of a big deal when you suddenly have a baby to take care of too. Even before he or she is born, once your partner is pregnant you are likely to be spending a lot more time at home. For some, your house or flat will not be big enough for the two of you and a baby, and adding a house move to the other stresses associated with pregnancy will be a necessary evil. Make sure, if you are moving, that you do it sooner rather than later, or you will be carrying the sofa and washing machine all by yourself! The most popular reason for moving, not surprisingly, is lack of space.

Steve said that although they were not in a position to move house, the pregnancy meant that he and his partner were forced to reconsider their one-bedroom flat. In the end they built a partition wall and simply converted their flat into a two-bedroom property; a relatively inexpensive and pragmatic solution, although they will have to move as soon as number two comes along. It is also worth bearing in mind that for the first few months, and often for up to a year or so, most babies, for very practical reasons, sleep in the same bedroom as their parents. So if you are not in a position to move or even to reorganize your living arrangements, don't worry too much. Baby will not be demanding a customized Thomas The Tank Engine bedroom for quite a few years yet.

Are We Safe?

Another very common desire was to move out of dense urban areas into a more rural or at least a more suburban setting. Suddenly, with a pregnancy, your reasons for living in the big city are turned upside down. You start to realize that being in close proximity to a selection of local pubs, restaurants, theatres and nightclubs is no longer such a priority; after all, are you ever going to get the chance to enjoy any of the above, ever again?! You chose your current home to satisfy your previous situation – maximising your enjoyment as a couple. Now you are (about to be) a family you would be much better off being within walking distance of a park or a good school, rather than the 24-hour drive- thru.

Fears about safety often emerge for the first time. Whilst you or your partner may not have had any previous worries about using dark subways and alleyways to get home before, suddenly with a baby *in utero* there is a very real fear. Exactly who else does share a home in your apartment block? Who are your neighbours? Why are those kids loitering around the off-license? (Forgetting, of course, that not so long ago you were buying 'street merchandise' from said kids.) Sometimes these fears will only be quelled by a complete change of location.

Becoming a parent must be one of the most common catalysts for radical life changes in terms of jobs and homes, and even the country you live in. Whatever you are considering, remember it should be a joint decision with your partner and make sure she is entirely happy with it.

DIY

You've been avoiding it for years, but those little jobs will be staring you in the face. Not to mention that you are likely to be getting subtle reminders from your partner about finishing the spare room, the kitchen tiles and the creaky floorboards. Over the next nine months, your weekends will no longer be a day in front of the television watching the football (probably good preparation for life with a new-born) but instead a life of wearing overalls with a paint roller in hand.

For many of the fathers interviewed, a resounding memory of their partner's pregnancy is the constant DIY involved in preparation for the new baby. It must be stressed that a number of dads said that many of the DIY tasks were of their own choosing. Others, though, recalled how it was strongly suggested that they get a bloody move on with the work. One father admitted to becoming a man 'possessed' with DIY. He felt and wanted to be, completely immersed in refurbishing the house in preparation for the baby. It was his way of becoming involved in the pregnancy, and his tangible efforts were rewarding and highly practical. The motivation behind his work was to ensure that they could maximise the selling price of the house, as they desperately wanted to move before the baby was born. Months of a full day's work in the office, followed by a night's work painting every room, paid off; they hassled the estate agent to speed up the process and were safely installed in their new home with two months to spare before the new arrival.

Nine months is not a long time in terms of weekends and therefore the work needs to begin in earnest almost from the outset. Certainly the longer you leave it, the more likely it is that you will be doing all the work on your own!

Shopping For Baby

Lisa and I were unstoppable. Here were two people, dead against retail therapy, getting up early on a Saturday to drive to the shops. Our hatred of the shopping culture no longer mattered; there was a baby coming and that child was going to get everything she needed; at whatever cost. I even hunted on the internet for baby merchandise and found a lot of what I needed there ... plus a lot more that I did not.

One set of grandparents bought the pushchair and another got the highchair. We countered by buying an expensive cot and bedding. Lisa and I would almost compete with each other to purchase 'surprises', each bought during our respective lunch hours. Colour themes become obsessive; cost was no longer an issue.

'Damn it! I'll have that Egyptian cotton blanket and matching pillowcase even if it bankrupts me!'

I tried and failed to pass off my pre-order of the (then) new Playstation 2 console as an essential purchase for our embryonic child. With any luck Alia would be a few weeks late, allowing me to complete Metal Gear Solid II before I would have to change my first nappy. Alia *was* a little late – a small matter of two weeks to be precise but Metal Gear Solid II's release date slipped by a year, by which time, the thought of getting an animated psycho to navigate numerous sets of stairs onboard a ship that seemed randomly controlled seemed uncannily similar to my own life at the time … thus the game was a flop in my eyes.

You will have already noticed the cost of ancillary items, such as pregnancy books and courses that you may have attended. Some of you will already be buying clothes, toys and hardware for your new baby. But it is the ongoing costs that will really take you by surprise. Nappies and all the associated paraphernalia cost a lot. In fact, bank on thousands just for nappies, for the first two years alone. Although babies don't eat a lot, certainly initially, providing for an extra mouth still costs money. For instance, just how many butternut squashes, pumpkins and sweet potatoes do you currently buy? None? You will very soon be introduced to vegetables you didn't even know existed.

Stuff You 'Need' To Buy

You will read the magazines and believe the advertising too. The amount of stuff you will feel you have to buy in preparation for your baby is unbelievable. There's the special bin for new-born's nappies; each one will be processed in this contraption so that you will be left with a string of nappy-sausages, all fragranced in that odd, nappy-sack smell. It will be a matter of only three months or so before the nappies become too big for the bin to cope. They're not cheap, either!

How trendy do you want to be when it comes to pushchairs? There are the three-wheel varieties; some even have a hand-operated brake and a bell. Or there's the standard four-wheel chassis, with its eight chunky wheels. Do you go for an aerodynamic, minimalist look or for something that would be more suited to mounting an offensive in the desert?

Chances are, by the time the two of you, both sets of parents, not to mention pre-uncles, pre-aunties and both sets of friends, get involved you'll have at least one of everything for every day of the week. You've seen the bibs that name each day of the week; how about impressing the local parent-and-toddler group with a different chariot for the baby, every time you come for tea and biscuits?

Grows On Trees, Does It?

However, it's best not to get carried away. Adam came home from work a week after learning from his partner that they were expecting their first child, to find the lounge brimming with a pram, a cot, several large stuffed toys and numerous sets of clothes. He wasn't disturbed so much about the items going on to his credit card as about the timing. A self-confessed fatalist, he had been reluctant to tell even his own parents about the pregnancy, never mind friends, until the three-month embargo had passed. Although not particularly superstitious, he felt it was tempting fate to indulge in so much consumerism, so early on. In utter disbelief he found brochures pertaining to the local independent schools and even a message on the answer- phone regarding a booking for the christening.

Although it would be unfair to dictate when items should be purchased (except maybe if it is all on your credit card!) the lesson to be learnt (isn't it always) is communication. Adam had a real fear of buying too much too soon, but hadn't actually mentioned it.

Top Gear

An Audi TT, although pretty nice to look at, is not really the most practical of cars when baby arrives. This is true of most sports cars, and anything in fact that does not have at least four seats and tons of room in the back.

The amount of stuff that you will need to carry around once your baby is born is tremendous. There's the pushchair, the baby seat, nappy bag, toys, bedding, food, more food, changes of clothes, sterilized bottles and maybe a travel cot or two. This stuff is bulky, heavy, and doesn't fold down much smaller than when it is erect – oh, and your baby, you and your partner have to fit in somewhere in between all of this.

You promised yourself that you would never stoop so low, but it is time to meet and be proud of the estate car. This is why they exist; *you* are who they were made for. They are deliberately painted in particularly drab colours and it is increasingly difficult to find the space to park one, but you will end up buying one just the same, and maybe even growing to like it. If it's any consolation, they tend to come with nippier engines nowadays. Yes, the motorbike will have to go. Sorry.

My Larder's Bigger Than Yours

One of your biggest expenses, along with the items that are directly attributable to the baby, will be the need for white goods. As a couple it is quite easy to cope with a visit to the launderette once a week, washing the dishes by hand, and living out of a fridge that is dwarfed by some hotel rooms' mini-bars. But when baby arrives this simply will not do. Your baby, certainly in the early months, will require numerous changes of clothes, every day. No matter how hard you try, their Babygros will be covered in puke, wee and poo. Your clothes will *also* be covered in puke, wee and poo, and no doubt any guest that comes to visit the little bundle of joy will not leave empty-handed either. Babies really aren't fussy; they'll mess up everything with their excretions, indiscriminately. A washing-machine is essential.

Your fridge will need to accommodate all of your food and your baby's. Usually this will mean a few bottles of pre-mixed milk in sterilized bottles, a few spare bottles and spare teats, and, as the child grows older, a fantastic selection of fresh fruit and vegetables. You will need an enormous fridge to store it properly and that probably means a different one to that which you are using now.

A dishwasher you can comfortably get away without, but the time you used to spend lovingly washing dishes whilst the other dried will be no more. There's going to be another nappy to change or bottle to make; anything that can maximize your time with your baby is an investment – if you have the space, get a dishwasher.

Gadget Man

Although you will want to make the house perfect in every respect, be careful when it comes to gadgets and furniture. There really is no point splashing out on a great new TV and soundbar, because within two years it will be unrecognizable. The TV screen, 4K or not, will have a generous coating of yoghurt over the screen and in the speakers; and the DVD player will be well acquainted with a slice of buttered toast that makes the tracking go haywire after about an hour. As far as gadgets are concerned, make do with what you have, or you will only have to replace the new stuff before you know it.

The same can be said for chairs and sofas. They get ruined. Not just tatty or a little bit stained on one cushion – absolutely trashed. Babies are amazing; so pleasant, yet so destructive. Save the money, buy an estate car and acknowledge that your trendy years are over.

3. Getting Jiggy With It

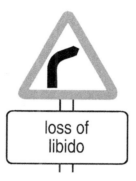

loss of
libido

Many men want a baby the same way they want a 1000cc motorbike. It would be a nice addition to the current set-up and, more importantly, so they believe, it will mean a tremendous amount of sex guaranteed for weeks, if not months. What could be better than that?

In fact, most men interpret the question, 'Would you like to have a baby' as a code meaning, 'So are you actually fertile?' Us blokes like a challenge and this is a challenge where we certainly wouldn't mind rising to the occasion. It's game-on and there are people watching (metaphorically, of course).

Did The Earth Move For You, Baby?

The planning of a pregnancy can make the whole issue of sex a bit confusing to the average bloke, and that's even before she's gotten pregnant. It's a general rule that as relationships become more serious and long-term, sadly sexual relations tend to become less frequent. Then, suddenly, you are going to make a baby together and you're both on sexual overdrive. After like what has seemed like a sexual drought there's an exhausting feast; the two of you can't get enough of each other. Soon after, you both watch your partner's first period come and go, but you try not to get too disheartened. If at first you don't succeed, try, try again. New techniques and positions are introduced; it's all good fun and you only wish you'd decided to do it earlier – it's fair to say that this having a baby lark is a lot of fun.

But, the focus can become 'clinical', especially in cases where a fertility programme is being followed. Sex becomes almost mechanical, especially if you employ any methods relating to ovulation, best times of day, or abstinence beforehand. We're a fickle lot sometimes and being asked to march to nature's beat can be like having a fridge full of T-Bone steaks and cold beers – some nights we would simply prefer a glass of wine and a slice of toast.

Many interviewees complained that their partners became pragmatic about conceiving. It was very much function over form and all the excitement of the early weeks had long since gone. Pragmatic sex can be horrid. A number of fathers interviewed complained that the quest for baby became like Arthur's search for the Holy Grail. Sex was taken over by pregnancy, which seemed unobtainable. To add insult to injury, the news and soaps would always be full of teenage pregnancies. What exactly were these youngsters doing to get up the duff so easily? Painful viewing, when all the two of you really want is for one sperm, one of the hundreds of millions that have been despatched in the past few months to hit the target.

Wishful Thinking

It's a sad fact that, generally, bloke's fantasies and turn-ons tend to be a bit pervy. Many of us like the idea of receiving oral sex, or a quickie, fully clothed on the sofa before work. There are fantasies involving multiple women; one of my personal favourites includes 10 bikini-clad young ladies on a yacht – but I digress ... My point is that very few of us fantasize about the missionary position, with our partners, at precisely 7.20a.m., a week on Tuesday. Yet this is what sex often becomes; an appointment or a goal-orientated meeting contrived and premeditated to the point where you would rather, quite honestly, prefer to amuse yourself in the bathroom for five minutes, thank you very much.

Plus, you probably had to clean up your act to ensure that your sperm had the best chance possible; so all the drugs, beer and cigarettes that you may have once enjoyed are now off limits. Masturbation is, most definitely, a cardinal sin. Just when you might need some, or all, of these methods of 'release', they are denied. It's true that the end justifies the means, but none of us react well to frustration. And it can be very frustrating if you don't get the results you desire. Some men reported feeling like they'd become just a piece of machinery in the baby-making project. Many felt they'd failed.

The more months that pass the more anxious you can become. If you are trying to conceive with third-party assistance, such as IVF, then the cost of a missed cycle and the heartache of having to explain your 'failure' are as hard to digest as the lack of results. At some stage or another we all wish we had shares in the companies that make pregnancy kits. They're not cheap and the only thing that is worse than disappointment is being made to pay for disappointment. All these factors can play havoc with a man's virility.

Mark reported in his interview that his wife had read a book that told her how to ensure they had a boy. The gist of the preparation was that he had to refrain from beer, cigarettes and red meat for extended periods of time. The key to ensuring you were creating a boy was a build-up of sperm, so sex was incredibly infrequent and he was absolutely forbidden from 'enjoying his own company'. They stuck to the rules (unwillingly on his part) and a baby was conceived – a beautiful girl.

However it happened, the fact that you are reading this book means that sooner or later you were successful in your quest for a baby and the words, 'I'm pregnant' were spoken. As I mentioned earlier, sometimes the news of the pregnancy can be almost an anticlimax. 'Oh, that's nice,' you respond rather than, 'Darling, that's fantastic.' Another reason for this could be that what once was fun had begun to feel like a bit of a chore; you had almost lost sight of the objective. At least the 1000cc motorbike would have been as exciting every time you rode it, no matter what time of the day or night.

Three In A Bed

The most conclusive findings from the interviews I conducted were regarding sex during pregnancy. To all the other questions, answers differed widely. When it came to sex, fathers found themselves in one of two distinct camps – those who maintained sexual activity with their partners comparable to that of pre-pregnancy, and those who most definitely did not. The shift in attitudes to sex during pregnancy is not just something that happens to your partner; most men begin to think a little differently about the whole process too. Obviously there is no possibility of injuring your unborn child, but for the more arrogant among us, myself included, it does cross your mind at least once.

These camps were roughly the same size – there was an equal number of fathers who said that their sexual relations remained pretty much the same and those who said they did not. So, as a ballpark figure, you have about a 50 per cent chance that things will be as good as before the pregnancy, at least for the next few months.

In one extreme case, a father was told by his partner that it was medically recommended not to have sex until at least the third trimester. By the time the embargo had been lifted, it had become too uncomfortable for her anyway. I suspect that the nine months of his partner's pregnancy seemed to pass a lot slower for him than most.

Be Sensitive

It is best to be prepared for possibilities such as your partner going completely off sex for the entire pregnancy and for some months after the birth. Deep down you will appreciate that this is not a conscious decision just to wind you up and pay you back for getting her into her current state, but something caused by the pregnancy. She still likes it as much as you, just not at this present juncture. Trying times indeed.

The major reason why your partner might go off sex is simply exhaustion; this is especially true in the first and third stage of pregnancy. Although her sex drive might be as high as yours, it's not much good to either of you if she's flat out asleep on the sofa by the time you get home from work.

Martin's wife Annie was unfortunate enough to feel dreadful throughout most of her pregnancy. She had terrible morning sickness almost from the outset, which everyone assured her would calm down after the first three months.

Six months on and she was still constantly nauseous. Not keeping any food down, coupled with intense exhaustion, meant that sex – the evil act that had got her into this abysmal state in the first place – was most definitely not on the menu. Martin found it hard not to feel personally rejected by Annie's unresponsiveness, despite the rational part of his brain telling him to chill out. Neither enjoyed the nine months much at all. However, they were so entranced by the end result that they were foolhardy enough to do it all again. And pregnancy number two turned out to be entirely different – Annie went into sex overdrive. She felt 'like a cat on heat', kept grabbing Martin in compromising places and even admitted to lusting after young men in the local supermarket. A little embarrassing when you're a 35- year-old mum wearing outsize maternity sweatpants covered with rusk stains. The point is, you never can tell which way the sex issue is going to go.

Whatever your partner's reaction to sex during pregnancy, remember that you were instrumental in bringing this new status quo into play. Try to respect her need for rest and show affection without it necessarily leading on to sex. And if you are being denied and feel particularly horny all the time, it is likely that you will become fairly well reacquainted with a favourite pastime you thought you had left behind as a teenager.

Pamela And Her Five Sisters

Whether sex is actually on the cards or not, you will probably be thinking about it much more often than usual. Pregnancy can be, quite frankly, frustrating, and in a bid to keep tempers controlled, you might find yourself perusing the top shelf of the local newsagents for the first time since school. Your partner may or may not react kindly to you logging on to porn sites full of nubile

nubile young women, who are, it would appear, certainly not heavy with child. It is not recommended that you ask her to comment on the 'actresses', or that you suggest she might like to participate in the home video section at this particular juncture. It will be your clandestine relationship between man and hand that sustains you – perfectly normal and highly rewarding. Happy reading.

Me, Male

Impregnating one's partner, for many men, brings out their alpha male. Along with the grin and the pride comes the feeling of strength and fertility. You have achieved something commonplace, yet exclusive. New mums often talk of being welcomed into a kind of 'club' when they announce that they are pregnant. I don't think it differs for men. It is a club you have joined and may rejoin as many times as you like. The feeling of pride at being a father lasts not just for the length of the pregnancy but right through your child's life. It is both exciting and a relief to find out that you're in full working order. Let's face it; most men at one stage or another wonder if they're 'firing blanks'.

Sexual Tyrannosaurus

They say that pregnant women tend to dream and think of sex more often than they did before the pregnancy; whether this manifests into actually activity is another issue entirely. Many men think more often of sex too. I suppose it is back to that alpha male in us all – we've successfully managed to make our partner pregnant, so why stop there? The urge to continue to 'spread our seed' is fantastically strong. It is as though we have a mission to populate the planet all by ourselves. Obviously, most of us do not act on these urges but you will probably feel incredibly virile and constantly horny.

At the same time, your changing relationship with your partner may make you feel insecure and this may manifest itself in a feeling of wanton lust. When this is coupled with a break or a change in sexual relations, it seems that many men (albeit for a few moments) feel a sudden desire to prove their fertility again and again. Although those I spoke to all stressed that they did not and would not actually fulfil their fantasies, they did start actively to fancy other women. Any 'standards' that a man would ordinarily judge a woman by seemed to go completely out the window. Big bum, little bum, six bums, it no longer mattered – if we were a little less moral, and were given half a chance, it seems that many of us for a few weeks, would want to shag everyone.

Quite simply, far from being put off sex, you might want it more than ever before. Your unborn child is testimony to your virility; everything is working properly and your partner's womb is bearing witness to the fact! You might, on occasion, have to check yourself from swaggering down the road like John Wayne. This feeling of virility can continue after the birth when you proudly push your baby's pushchair into the unsuspecting backs of pedestrians' ankles. It's a huge ego-boost when a passing stranger checks out your partner's bump: 'I did that,' you will proudly say to yourself. Experiences like that epitomize, for many, what it means to be a man.

When Thoughts Turn To Actions

And then there are the occasions when men stray during their partner's pregnancy. These tend not to be full-blown affairs that last for any length of time but instead opportunistic mistakes that can and do lead to complete disaster. Onlookers might argue that it is the worst time someone could choose to be unfaithful, and onlookers would be right. But realistically it might also be the most likely time for it to occur.

We may feel a lot hornier now that our partner is pregnant and consequently more frustrated – a difficult combination. It would also be accurate to say that some women are attracted to men who have proven themselves by fathering a baby – even if that baby is still *in utero*. Combined with the father's increased awareness of sexuality, virility and fertility, if said dad is to have a few too many drinks with said woman, then it could lead to a very naughty (and very stupid) night indeed.

Avoid this route like the plague, no matter how tempted you might be. The fallout is huge and it is three lives you will be ruining, not just one. Log on to PornHub, have a wank, and enjoy Julie, 23, from Coventry – let's face it, the fantasy is probably a lot better than the drunken pick-up in the pub. Plus, you won't have to buy her six house doubles and a pack of bacon fries to get your wicked way.

Seriously though, keep it zipped, and if it has crossed your mind so much as once, don't put yourself in situations any more where you might be tempted. Isn't there someone sitting at home with your baby growing inside of them, who would be thankful for your company? Think about it.

Will I Still Fancy It?

Let's be honest here, much as we adore our partners and glory in their fecundity, most men's ideal pin-up does not have a stomach that dwarfs all her other attractions. Just try and remember that you are not the only one in the relationship who is aware of this – most women have a critical enough view of their own bodies already, and certainly do not need to feel insecure about their sexuality at this particular time. A little sensitivity will go a very long way. Leching over the nubile young presenters on Saturday morning telly (the girls that is, not Ant and Dec) is not going to go down too well while your beloved is shuffling back from the loo in her maternity kaftan, having just barfed up most of her breakfast (again).

There are two distinct camps when it comes to the sexiness of pregnant women; those who found their pregnant partners even more incredible and sexually desirable, and those who, frankly, didn't. If you are lucky enough to be one of the former, and your partner is also feeling very much in the groove, both of you are going to benefit from a lot of added extras during this period.

Big, Bouncy And Shiny

Let's start from the top. If you're lucky, it's like she's just stepped out of the salon. Something profound will happen to your partner's hair three months or so in. With a toss of the coin, you will either be introduced to a new fuller, richer and bouncier head of hair or you will become acquainted with the lank, oily, in-need-of-a-bit-of-a-wash look. Both results are completely normal and both will prove to be yet another visible sign that the pregnancy is progressing well. Whether it is bounce or lank for you, your partner's hair will become darker, but if she is someone who is quite prone to dyeing her hair anyway, you could be forgiven for not noticing.

Coupled with the change in hair often comes the fuller cheeks and the celebrated 'glow' of pregnancy. Your partner's skin will seem smoother, and any little wrinkles may also disappear (though it's probably best not to mention this – she might take it as a backhanded compliment). Her cheeks may even shine, as if they are now a beacon to fertility. Combined, it is a remarkable and often glorious transformation.

Oh. And it's not just the hair on the head that grows … a few of the fathers' interviewed were rather surprised when they were introduced to their partner's new hairy belly and, don't cringe, nipples. In these cases, theirpartners had dark hair and were expecting boys – apparently this was due to the baby's testosterone causing all sorts of con- fusion in the woman's body.

'Your hairy chest is so, so … much more impressive than mine!'

Beautiful, Beautiful Breasts

Quite early on in pregnancy, you can expect your partner to receive a visit from the so-called 'breast fairy', officially known as engorgement. I don't think that you will ever see or even hear the word associated with anything other than breasts (except maybe penises) but isn't it a fantastic word! It suggests immense size, much more positively than, for example, 'big' or 'large'. Engorged is what your partner's breasts will look like, and for her (and hopefully you), exactly how they will feel.

Thanks to man's new best friend, colostrum, your partner's breasts will defy gravity and often belief. You will bear witness to your partner transcending the alphabet in cup sizes, all within a matter of weeks. To begin with this new size is matched with new sensitivity, which may make boobs a no-go area as far as you are concerned. Unfortunately it is my experience, and the experience of many of the fathers interviewed, that the old maxim of 'look, but don't touch' will be employed almost at the same moment that your partner's ample breasts, become, well, ampler. Thankfully, the tenderness of these new wondrous objects passes after a few months, and there should be many weeks during the middle part of pregnancy when they can be fully appreciated by you and your partner. It may be that your partner expresses annoyance at her new larger breasts, and feigns resentment at any Pamela Anderson comparisons, but this is probably more to do with the cost of replacing bras than displeasure at having bigger boobs. If you and your partner are both lucky enough to be experiencing a heightened sexual drive during the second trimester, then you will already be planning your fifth, if not sixth child, eager to do everything to maintain this Nirvana-esque status quo. You will both have a limited window of opportunity on this one, so enjoy it while you can.

For most women the transformation is very sudden. You will probably be hoping that the larger size will be retained after birth, and certainly if your partner is planning to breastfeed for any length of time this will indeed be the case – wasted, alas, because any fondling usually causes the glands to spurt milk across the room. You may find this very amusing but you will be denying your baby her essential midnight meal. Once breastfeeding is replaced with solids, your partner's breasts will return to their pre-pregnancy state. Life is just not fair.

Sexy Undies?

The extra weight and girth of the breast will mean many shopping expeditions for new bras over the months. This may sound exciting but unfortunately maternity bras tend to be neither flattering in themselves, nor of what they contain
– they are a pragmatic solution, where function very much overrides form. Sorry chaps, but prepare yourselves for the nursing bra, which apart from maternity briefs is possibly the single most unattractive piece of clothing available to womankind. These 'contraptions' are obviously a necessity. You know that they're horrid, and no doubt your partner knows they're horrid too. Laugh about it.

One father I interviewed had been sent off to John Lewis to buy two nursing bras. Suffering from a severe lack of sleep, looking unkempt and feeling a tad awkward, he roamed around the underwear section like a zombie for almost an hour, followed closely by a suspicious security guard. When confronted, he blurted out in defence that he was 'looking for maternity bras – for his wife.' Immediately the mood of the assistants changed. Smiles came to their faces and a knowing, sympathetic look crossed all their faces. Whilst they laughed and joked at his obvious embarrassment, they were incredibly helpful and made sure the experience was over quickly. This is one of the big contradictions of pregnancy – although it's a hugely personal thing it is also incredibly public; by the end of the experience you will be discussing your partner's bits and ailments with the mastery of an experienced doctor.

The Backside

At times you will feel like one, but more importantly, the bottom that you share a house with is likely to get bigger and louder.

'Does my bum look big in this?' is a question often posed to blokes. Let's face it, us connoisseurs of this most attractive part of the female anatomy know instinctively what makes a great bum. (I just can't get you out of my mind, Kylie …)

But not even the most self-conscious of pregnant women would dare ask this question when pregnant. They know, without a shadow of a doubt, that the answer is yes. And so will you. Big and little bums just get bigger. There's no hiding from it and there's no avoiding it. Your partner's body knows perfectly well where to stick the extra pounds and those two cute, perfectly-shaped, round little cheeks of fun are the perfect host.

Annoyingly for women, the big bum often precedes the big belly, which can be a little disconcerting. It will go away after birth and can be a lot of fun for you in the meantime. And if your partner didn't gain weight there would be something seriously wrong – not just with her but also with your unborn baby. This is not a time for the Atkins Diet.

In some respects, experiencing Lisa pregnant was the nearest I have come to having an affair. You're familiar with the general rules, but some things have changed so fundamentally that it is like enjoying a whole new woman. 'Whole', of course, being the operative word.

Leaving His Or Her Mark

Like a chameleon, your partner's skin will change its appearance, right across her body. Whilst you will hopefully not see bright shades of green, orange or yellow, you may well become accustomed to red and eventually white lines appearing in various places on your partner's body. Stretch marks are, more than anything else (apart from maybe a toddler dangling from her arm or the scar of a Caesarean), your partner's major lasting reminder that she is now, and will always be, a mother. In essence they are a battle wound, proof of the deed, and though they will eventually fade to almost nothing, they are a lasting visible reminder of what actually happened during pregnancy.

The very sudden (in relative terms), drastic change in your partner's body size and shape due to junior growing means that she will almost certainly develop stretch marks, to one extent or another. These pencil-thin lines are her skin's reaction to suddenly being, and, as the name suggests, stretched to the limits of excess. Stretch marks will appear on the areas of her body that alter the most, namely around the stomach and breasts and, to a lesser degree, around her bottom and legs. After witnessing one birth, I am convinced that all mothers deserve a medal or award of some description. Although most women do not initially equate stretch marks with an accolade, after their initial horror most agree that it is a small price to pay, and many even now bear their marks, as a warrior should, with pride.

Touch And Taste

You may also notice ever-so-slight changes in the tone, or more accurately the pigment, of your partner's skin. No, your partner hasn't regressed to teenage years, but she may become a bit spotty during pregnancy. It's those hormones running rampant again and a few spots on the face are a common reaction. They won't last and they are of course harmless, just a bit disconcerting for your partner if she is pushing 30 and thought she'd left spots behind with her virginity a decade ago.

Ok, back to breasts now, a favourite topic of mine.

Expect your partner's nipples and surrounding areas to become both darker and bigger, no matter what their pre- pregnancy size. Combined with the breast engorgement, it really is a sight to behold, and not one that most of us are adverse to. Along with the breast size, the nipples and aureole (area surrounding the nipples) will shrink back after the pregnancy, but it appears that the change in colour is permanent. Not an unpleasant one, but definitely noticeable.

Then, for those of you who enjoy exploring some Latin terminology in the bedroom, there is a good chance that your partner's pregnancy may also create an interesting array of scents and flavours in her most private of places. For most of the fathers interviewed, any new odours or tastes were not a concern for others, the changes were a little distracting. As with most things, it is a delicate subject that is best discussed with your partner. Each individual is, well, individual, and therefore there are no hard-and-fast rules.

Finally, a most odd change that may occur to your partner's body is the 'Linea Nigra' or 'runway', which appears as a perfectly symmetrical line from her belly- button to the top of her pubic hair, as if it were a visual guideline for the baby to follow on his or her way out. This inexplicable path of colour embarrasses, yet at the same time fascinates, many an observer. The 'dirty line to happiness', as I dubbed it, is not uncommon and will last long after your baby is born. It's a curious phenomena, yet another 'mark' of motherhood for your partner.

Losing Your Mojo

There are men who have admitted to losing all desire for sex once they learnt that their partners were pregnant.

There are any number of reasons why this might happen, almost all of them psychological. Suddenly finding your partner, the partner you loved enough to want to have a baby with, sexually unattractive is very unlikely to happen. Some men worry about hurting the child or their partner. Some fathers mentioned that they were put off sex because, no matter how ridiculous it seemed, they couldn't help but feel that their baby was listening; able to understand what was going on, and in some way to disapprove of his or her parent's actions. Much as we cannot imagine our own parents having sex, we certainly do not even want to imagine being caught having sex by our kids.

One of the most common reasons for going off sex is the change in our perception of our partner. Until the pregnancy we were used to seeing as a sexual being, maybe even a bit naughty. Now she is on a pedestal – a mother figure that needs to be protected (from us as much as outside influences). Or maybe we had a troubled relationship with our own mother and mixed feelings about this suddenly kick in to the mix. Emotional changes in us may outweigh the physical changes in partners. We sometimes begin to treat them differently – with kid gloves.

It must be stressed that it is not just women that lose the desire (albeit temporarily) for sex following birth. A few interviewees were incredibly honest about their own worries and doubts on this subject. For some men, the way they perceived their partner, now a mother-to-be, had altered. The days of quickies in the lounge, or even someone else's lounge, were behind them. This pinnacle of womanhood who they were honoured to share a new life with was too important to trouble with their own dirty desires.

If you are put off sex for a period do try to find out the reasons and explain why, or you will certainly upset your partner. She will find it much easier to accept that you have madonna/whore issues than that you find her maternity knickers a turn-off. And worry not, eventually your sexual desire will return, maybe not at exactly the same time as hers, but it will.

Putting The Kama Into Sutra

As the months of pregnancy increase, the number of sexual positions possible decreases. Although usually obvious, your concept of what is still possible might vary wildly from your partner's, so it is probably best to check anything with her first – athletic variety may have to wait until your baby is fast asleep in a cot in a few months time. Some interviewees mentioned that they received oral sex more than usual during the months of pregnancy, which satisfied their needs. All I can say is that I wouldn't ask if it's not forthcoming, as the idea might not 'go down' too well with some partners.

Although there are numerous variants, and I am sure that the two of you will enjoy exploring the opportunities, you are going to be limited to three main sexual positions from about the second trimester onwards. The missionary position (thankfully, for some of us) is now out of bounds as it will place too much pressure on the womb and therefore your partner's bladder. Listed in no particular order of preference are your new options:

'It's Your Birthday' – From Behind may well be the most comfortable position for your partner. Other than the essential, there is little physical contact and, therefore, no matter how slight and svelte you might think you are, you will not be making her uncomfortable by adding your weight to her abdominal area. Some dads who admitted to not being completely at ease with the ever-growing bulge found that 'the position with a view' was ideal for both partners.

'Ride On' – Her On Top works fine for most couples at the best of times. During pregnancy it may well be a necessity. Again, no pressure on the womb and what an incredible view, my friend. Engorged breasts, bulging tum, and hair cascading over her face and shoulders – a beautiful sight. Unlike the previous position, however, both of you may not have as much control when it comes to actual depth of penetration and your time with her in the 'driving seat' may be limited.

'Lazy Sunday' – Spooning is a lovely way to fall asleep together (at least until your arm falls asleep, causing no small amount of pain) and can be a very gentle and non- obtrusive way to enjoy sex during pregnancy. Once again, you will not be adding pressure on the womb (there's a pattern here, isn't there) and your partner will much prefer lying on her side as opposed to her front or back. It might not be the most energetic position in your repertoire, but that's not the point, is it?

It's Hard For Her

Stretchmarks, hairy nipples, engorged breasts, three extra stones to heft around and a waddling fat belly – she may or may not mention it, but to one degree or another your partner's sexual confidence will take a knock during pregnancy. No matter how much you feel your partner has changed now that she is a mother-to-be, rest assured that she feels it a million times more. At the risk of sounding like a broken record, be sensitive and be loving. After all, you're hardly perfect yourself …

When it comes to sex after the birth, as well as the physiological reasons that will prevent it for a while there may be some psychological issues to sort out. Your partner's body has suffered a massive trauma and will need time to heal and recover, regardless of whether your child was born 'naturally' or by caesarean section.

You probably witnessed the event too, so it's not as if you are unsympathetic about the situation.

Certainly for the first few days you will both be so engrossed in looking at and caring for your new baby that, the last thing on either of your minds will be sex. However, there will come a point, be it days, weeks or even months (?) later when your mind and body will be ready for sex again. The question is, will hers? The simple answer is no, probably not. Just give it time.

How Was It For You?

Is sex any different after the birth? Yes and No. It's the same act, with the same person, using the same parts and the same techniques; but everything has changed … or at least it has as far as your thoughts are concerned. There is a myth that the vagina will not return to its pre-birth size; it will. Several fathers interviewed even claimed that their partners had been so enthusiastic with their pelvic floor exercises after the birth, they could always fall back on a career as a Thai brothel performer if times got too hard. Generally, the only difference is purely psychological, for both of you, and getting back on top of things, so to speak, will prove me right.

If you do have any worries about your partners vagina being different, bear in mind that she will have the same fears, only magnified, and a bit of subtlety is the order of the day on this one. Early attempts at sex after the birth of your child may be awkward in comparison to your carefree days of yore — the emphasis will be very much on you being gentle.

Less Of Those Antics, Young Man

Of course, once the birth is over and your partner is back to her old self it will be business as usual ... or will it? Getting up constantly through the night combined with the stress of learning how to cope with a new baby (especially if there are already children in the family to attend to) can be draining on both partners. This is a huge issue for most women and is most definitely where you should play more of a supportive role and less of the clown. Be prepared: no matter how supportive you think you have been, and I am sure you will do a great job, your early advances may well be gently refused:

'Stick that thing anywhere near me and you will be sleeping on the sofa.'

'Please?'

'I've had four hours sleep in about as many days. No, I don't want a shag thanks very much.'

'Please?'

'No! Oh, would you mind fetching me another puke rag; this one's sodden. And it's bin day tomorrow, take the bags out please.'

But don't worry, before you know it you'll be trying for number two. All good things come to those who wait.

4. The 1st Trimester

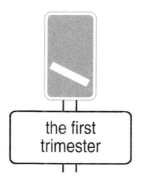

the first
trimester

... Or How Your Life Just Got Turned Upside Down

In all the guidebooks for women, the midwives and doctors break things down into the three trimesters of pregnancy. I have done so too, where necessary. These handy, bite-size periods of time clearly delineate the separate and distinct stages that your partner will experience. As a rule of thumb the trimesters last for approximately three months each. Therefore, the first trimester covers month one to the end of month three – or weeks one to eleven.

In our own way, I think us blokes experience three trimesters too. The first is the most radical: it usually hits us like a banana, swung by a particularly aggressive orang-utan, right between the eyes. We are left in what we initially perceive to be 'a bit of a mess'.

Finding out you are going to be a father is shocking, tremendous and overwhelming. The hard bit is trying to stop thinking about yourself 'How will I cope? I'm not ready for this!' and getting down to the business of supporting your partner. Like most things, easier said than done.

Who's A Moaning Michael?

Both of you will be. During the first trimester your partner's moods will swing (like the largest of pendulums) as a direct result of her pregnancy hormones. And yours will too. In some ways the first trimester is the worst; there is so much for you both to get used to. The first three months of the pregnancy will also have the most dramatic emotional effect on your partner. She will seem lethargic and forgetful, confused and weepy, occasionally very sick yet often intensely happy. Not dissimilar to you yourself really, (maybe without the weepy bit), but it's always horrible looking in the mirror first thing in the morning or late at night.

Early pregnancy is a time of very mixed emotions. In one respect you will almost want to stand there with a measuring tape, witnessing the physical growth of your partner's tummy as it happens. Paradoxically, you might also arrange to go off for a weekend with some friends, having entirely forgotten that your partner is now carrying your child. Sorry Lisa, but Sweden was lots of fun if that helps!

Us bloke's commonly underestimate the power and ferocity of the changes that pregnancy brings, both to us and our partners as individuals, and to the dynamic of the relationship. But seeing is believing, as they say, and it will soon become crystal clear what a profound act bringing a child into the world really is. The physical changes may involve only her, but the emotional changes will involve both of you.

As well as coming to terms with pregnancy and father- hood, you will also have to come to terms with your new temporary partner. This is the 'twin sister' syndrome mentioned earlier; so much remains familiar yet so much is alien. The early stages of pregnancy can, and probably will, really affect your mood. Sadly, you will not be able to cite hormonal changes as an excuse; tempers will become fraught and harsh words may even be exchanged – but never fear, the second trimester is usually far more serene. Recognizing that this is a stressful time is winning half the battle.

More Tests Than An International Cricket Team

Your partner will have to lose any inhibitions she might have about her body, because over the next nine months she will see myriad people who are intent on seeingparts of her that were hitherto reserved for you, and you only. Over the course of the pregnancy your partner will be tested, prodded, poked and examined many more times than she will care to remember. It is quite a public spectacle being pregnant in the twenty-first century.

Most tests will be carried out by ultrasound scan, or on your partner's blood and urine. Ultrasound scans can be used any time from the fifth week of the pregnancy through to delivery. Many women have their first scan at around 12 weeks, or towards the end of the first trimester, others at between 18 and 20 weeks. This may be the first time you will get to see your baby *in utero*. Though you won't be able to discern very much at all, other than a kind of pod sprouting arms and legs, this can be an incredibly emotional experience for many men, and the first time the pregnancy actually becomes 'real' to them. At this scan the doctor will give your partner her estimated 'due date' based on measurements of the foetus. This is D-day, a bit of a moveable feast (according to some studies only 4 per cent of babies actually arrive on their due date), but nevertheless one that you and your partner will have etched in your minds.

It's Life, But Not As We Know It

There are many reasons for using scans and they can change throughout the pregnancy – apart from just generally checking everything routinely, perhaps your partner has problems during the pregnancy or the doctor wants to check whether she is carrying twins, or perhaps she has certain medical conditions. Scans are perfectly safe; they ensure that the foetus is growing well and that there is enough amniotic fluid surrounding the baby. They can also be the first indication that there could be some complications with the pregnancy or the developing baby.

An ultrasound scan works by bouncing high-frequency sound waves off the foetus. The differing tissue types will cause the waves to bounce back in a different way. Thus, the monitor shows you a pictorial image of what has happened to those sound waves, which forms as differing shades of grey into, believe it or not, an image of your child. Most of the fathers interviewed expressed disappointment with either the screen image or the printout of their child. In Alia's scan her facial features came out very strongly, but her torso and legs were a complete blur.

It is at the scan that you may, depending on the policy of the Department or Local Health Authority, request to learn whether you are going to have a baby boy or a baby girl. Even if your wish is granted, it depends on the position and development of the foetus as to whether or not this will be possible. Although the result is usually correct, it can never be 100 per cent accurate.

It is usually possible to order prints of the scan. You often have to pay for them, which I personally think is a bit off, but we all end up doing so. Whether the quality of image is good or bad, I defy anyone not to start trying to see similarities between the baby's features and their own. 'Oh look, s/he has my chin' – I think not. I was guilty of digitally scanning the picture of the scan and posting it on the Internet, for the relations to see. I was so pleased to have something visual, something that confirmed that my baby was coming and that she was real. A word of advice from one of the interviewed dads – don't laminate the scan photo; it is printed on thermal paper and thus, when heated, the whole page turns black! If it was difficult to pick out your baby's features before, it will be impossible after that!

Is Everything OK?

It is usually towards the end of the first trimester or beginning of the second that doctors will, with your partner's agreement, start doing tests to make sure that everything is ok and the baby is developing in a normal, healthy way. As scans become ever more sophisticated there are many tests that your doctor can use them for, such as measuring the nuchal fold, a fold in the neck which can be a very early indication of Down's syndrome. Whatever the results of the early scans, your partner is probably not going to escape totally without having close encounters with a lot of blood and needles.

Blood is thicker than water, but by the time your partner's given her umpteenth blood sample, she's going to wish that it wasn't. One of the tests that your partner might choose, or be advised to have, is a blood test for alpha- fetoprotein when she is between 16 and 18 weeks pregnant. This test can be an early indicator for the risk of Down's syndrome, spina bifida or other neural tube defects. If the risk factors are above a certain level, she may go on to have more invasive tests such as Chorionic Villi Sampling (CVS), or amniocentesis. Her blood will also be tested to determine her blood group, iron levels, the presence of hepatitis B and Rhesus factor.

Another reason blood is tested is to assess haemoglobin levels to make sure that your partner is not anaemic. Haemoglobin levels will be checked again at 28 weeks and 36 weeks, but by this stage she will be an old hand at giving blood, and probably won't even look up from her pregnancy magazine during the appointment.

Important Decisions

The most alarming test for mum and dad is probably the CVS, which gives very accurate results and is becoming increasingly common. The test involves inserting a large needle through the abdomen or into the vagina to take out a piece of the placenta. The results are usually available about a week later. Despite being quite a nerve-racking experience it is a quick and straightforward procedure.

The whole issue of testing for possible problems with your baby is an increasingly emotive one. Some doctors argue that even by agreeing to the test you have already taken a step towards the possibility of aborting the pregnancy if there is anything seriously wrong. Not everyone will agree with this, however, and, as with most things in pregnancy, the important thing is to talk such issues through with your partner, and to support and respect her decisions.

You should try to accompany your partner for as many of these tests as you can. You may find them boring and inconvenient, but remember that for her they could be positively invasive, uncomfortable and highly undignified, not to mention emotionally traumatic. Just being the designated driver to and from appointments is an unglamorous but important role. If the results are in any way upsetting then you unquestionably do need to be there, both in a supportive and decision-making capacity. Although most tests are routine and will be, for you, as boring as going along to watch a session at the dentist, your presence can be hugely comforting. Your partner will have prepared herself for each of these tests and will know exactly what it is they are testing for, the procedure, the likely outcomes, and possibly even the statistics of success/failure for the last 150 years. You, on the other hand, will feel like a nodding dog most of the time. Bring a book! Unless, of course, you enjoy reading ten-year-old gossip magazines.

The Sight Of Blood

Blood plays a prominent role in the whole pregnancy and birth experience. As well as the number of samples your partner will have to provide throughout her pregnancy, there will be copious amounts about at the birth, and, on occasion, blood makes an unwelcome appearance during pregnancy also.

It must be stressed that the appearance of blood does not always mean miscarriage or problems, and some 'spotting', as it is called, is in fact quite common. But the appearance of blood is always a worry and not something that should be ignored. Your partner should always report it to her doctor or midwife. Spotting is light bleeding similar to, but lighter than, a typical period. It can occur at any time during the pregnancy but is most common in the early weeks, or toward the latter stages. There are many reasons for its occurrence for instance, when the fertilized egg attaches itself to the wall of the uterus, it can cause implantation bleeding, which is usually light and lasts a day or two. Spotting also takes place if your partner has a vaginal infection, or an irritated cervix. Toward the latter stages of pregnancy spotting can indicate that the placenta has broken away from the uterus or more commonly that the cervix is beginning to soften and even dilate – of course, this could actually be the beginning of labour … but we're jumping way ahead now.

Multiple Babies

Only one of my interviewees became a father to twins. He and his partner were well prepared for this as he had been one of a set of twins continuing a pattern that had always run in the family. The birth, however, still caused a significant shock. An over-zealous aunt had already bought them a pushchair (single seat) that had to be exchanged and it meant Granny had to knit two cardigans in the time left.

Multiple births are becoming more and more common, mainly due to various fertility treatments being employed, such as IVF. Preparing for the birth of twins or triplets is no different to preparing for the birth of a single child. Your partner will need the same support all the way through, if not more, and you will both have your hands full after the births. But looking at it positively, if you want a big family, expecting multiple babies speeds that whole process up!

The risk of birth defects in each twin will be somewhat higher than if your partner was expecting one baby, but this should not be cause for concern until something adverse actually occurs. Some women complain that the symptoms of pregnancy are amplified when expecting twins, especially with regard to morning sickness, mobility and swelling of the hands and feet.

It is unlikely that your partner will carry the twin pregnancy full term as it is generally accepted that she will go into premature labour (premature actually means before 37 weeks). Full-term pregnancy for a woman carrying twins is generally considered to be 38 weeks. The weight of the babies and the health of the mother will be very closely monitored. Put simply, the longer that the twins remain *in utero*, the better. A caesarean section will often be offered to older mums expecting twins, or if there is a history of complications during birth or of previous caesareans.

It is not so common any more for women expecting twins to be prescribed bed rest but it is likely that a doctor or midwife will suggest that they give up work before 28 weeks; it is possible to get a doctor's certificate supporting this which helps with regard to receiving benefits.

In Sickness And In Food Cravings

It's one of pregnancy's biggest clichés that your partner will experience morning sickness and food cravings. But there is nothing wrong if your partner doesn't suffer from morning sickness (count yourself and her lucky). Equally you shouldn't be overly concerned if she partakes in a little mid-afternoon snack consisting of soil fresh from the garden. Encourage her, insist everything is fine, nod, smile and store it up to tell your mates later. In fact, you should encourage cravings, occasionally. If your partner craves something quite easily accessible, like ice cream, buy a large tub of her favourite flavour and leave it in the freezer. Eating a couple of litres of chocolate ice cream probably isn't particularly nutritious, but it's hardly life-threatening either. And it's probably her body's way of telling her she needs more milk. At least, that's what she'll tell you.

If you are concerned about your partner's actual or potential weight gain, do not voice your worry. She will grow to an unbelievable size over the course of the coming months, and although you may at times be a little disturbed, make no references to harpoons. However difficult, it is important to remember that your partner's body is feeding and protecting your child: you should support her. During the entire pregnancy process, what you don't say can be as important as what you do. There is a time for rice salads and hours at the gym, and it is not now.

Everyone's experience is different. One father said that his wife had cravings for items of food that were incredibly expensive and that she was not allowed to eat, namely a particular type of un-pasteurized goat's cheese and sushi. In fairness to her she only cheated once – spectacularly, but luckily at her own financial expense.

Do You Have Deep-Fried Bananas?

If you have never seen 4.00 a.m. before, welcome to surreal- land. If you are lucky enough to be anywhere up to 20 miles away from a 24-hour supermarket, prepare to get very well acquainted, very soon. The items fathers have been despatched to buy vary from the mundane (bananas, jar of coffee, new potatoes, a red apple – not too waxy) to the obscure (ginger ale – not chilled, mojos, butternut squash, ice). Navigating the aisles early in the morning can be pretty hard, as the staff use the quiet hours to restock and the floor will be awash with packaging, spilt milk and general detritus that will pose a threat to you surviving to see your baby born. Not what you need at four in the morning and don't even dare to come home empty-handed! Unusual food cravings hold the same status during pregnancy as dirty nappies and sleepless nights hold once the baby is born. Some women even seem to be competing to have the strangest fixation – but perhaps that's unfair. Your partner's brain is incredibly clever; over the years it appears to have analysed everything that has been consumed and broken it down to a molecular level. So cravings for certain food types often relate to their specific properties. The brain decides that the body requires some additional vitamin C, so your partner eats fourteen oranges without breaking sweat. In fact citrus fruits were frequently mentioned in the interviews I conducted, either because the partner could no longer stand even the smell of them or because she would now comfortably consume a fresh lemon.

A few years ago I worked in an open-plan office with a lady who was pregnant. Every now and again we all saw her reaching into her drawer and surreptitiously munch on something; we couldn't quite work out what it was. A quick nibble or a lick and it would be thrust back into the drawer. Intrigued, we waited for said lady to go off to the loo, then had a peek in the drawer. It turned out that she was munching on a brick. I kid you not, a large chunk of house brick sat on top of a pile of compliment slips and the entire department's stock of ballpoint pens, and had tell-tale teeth marks all over it! I have since heard of similar example where someone began licking a chunk of coal – surely a daily iron tablet would have done the trick? The cause of such behaviour is low blood sugar and the old hormonal imbalance playing cheeky tricks. Not something to worry about, and for those of you in the city, 4.00 a.m. does offer the opportunity to drive on remarkably clear roads with no other cars or pedestrians (apart from very, very drunk people, still looking for their house, shouting 'Dave!').

As cravings are often a sign of being deficient in something, your partner's body recognizes this deficiency and hunts out what it needs from the most unlikely of sources. I find the brick story funny, but weird cravings should actually be reported to the doctor, as they may be a symptom of serious mineral deficiency.

Little Miss Fussy

Associated with cravings, but not to be mistaken for them, will be an increased fussiness about food. Many women will have difficulty keeping many hitherto favourites down. This can last for weeks or months. Your partner's sense of smell is now very finely attuned and inevitably her taste- buds are affected; this will lead to her finding solace in certain 'safe' foods that simply don't offend. Depending on your domestic situation you might find that you too suddenly eat a lot of the same thing (if *she* does the cooking), or you eat a lot of the same thing (if *you* do the cooking). Lisa's particular thing was for lamb. I am sure, given half a chance, she might have eaten one raw; luckily she wasn't in a fit state to bolt over a farmer's fence and catch one. I don't think that I have eaten lamb since the Millennium.

Morning Glory

On revealing our new father-to-be status, us blokes suffer endless references to dirty nappies and sleepless nights. The same will be happening to your partner with regards to morning sickness. Contrary to popular mythology, it is not a foregone conclusion. Some women get it bad, others get it good, and a poor few, get it every now and again. In some ways it is easier to know that you are going to suffer from it or remain untouched. The uncertainty is one of the most disconcerting things for many women.

Morning sickness is a misnomer in that it can, and often will, occur at all times of the day. For the vast majority, it is something that comes with the territory of the first trimester and then, abruptly, stops. For a few weeks Lisa suffered quite badly. There was a particular occasion when we were driving to work and I had to stop the car on an incredibly busy stretch of road next to a busy roundabout, gently mount the kerb, and throw open the passenger door so that Lisa could see her Weetabix again. I must mention that women get very good at both directional control and timing. With a quick wipe of tissue we were back on the road as if nothing out of the ordinary had occurred.

Morning sickness is caused by the sheer amount of hormones rushing around your partner's body. Despite popular misconception, the level of morning sickness she experiences does not, in any way, determine the sex of your baby or your partner's chances of miscarrying. In lucky cases it might be something suffered for a mere matter of weeks, if at all. In the more extreme cases morning sickness, or more accurately incredible and constant nausea, might last as long as six or seven months.

There's not really a lot you can do to help the situation, except maybe to be careful over what and when you cook, if you are that way inclined. I have to be honest and say that I remained tucked up in bed whilst most of Lisa's morning sickness was occurring; so the whole experience, other than a bit of fantastic driving on my behalf, missed me completely.

Most pregnant woman get very good at puking. Both Lisa and her friend Bev became Jedi masters and eventually got to the stage where they could puke, then carry on making the dinner, without breaking their rhythm. Apparently puking Weetabix out of your nose is not much fun. Your partner will learn to eat things that taste nice on the way up too. Weetabix is one of those things that doesn't!

My Wife, The Basset Hound

The most innocuous of smells or scents can have a powerful and even frightening effect on your pregnant partner. Lisa drinks a lot of tea; that is unless she is pregnant, when the stuff actually offends her. I found it amazing that somebody could go from numerous cups a day to zero, almost as soon as she became pregnant – it upset her even to go near the stuff; which, if nothing else, saved us a fortune in milk. With Alia busy growing inside her, the pleasant aroma of freshly cut grass or breakfast cooking that she had hitherto inhaled deeply into her lungs, led to dashes to the bathroom and intense vomiting. If you are a smoker, even though you will probably not be smoking in the house, just the scent of smoke clinging to your clothes will be terribly upsetting to your partner and her stomach. For a good few weeks, crossing the road might even be difficult. Your smoking might be hard enough to cope with, but the smell of exhaust fumes, hot tarmac or even the local fish and chip shop are enough to turn your partner physically green. The sense of smell and taste are so intertwined it is sometimes difficult to tell which is having the greater effect on your brain; this is true for your partner too, only exaggerated. Meat eaters complain that what would have been a lovely steak a couple of months before is now impossible to eat. The texture feels different in their mouth, the taste is more 'meaty' and the juices are far from appetising. Food lovers can become random in their diet, unable to eat the same-size portions as before, or not wanting to eat certain food types at all, yet equally being happy to scoff 16 mackerel fillets in one sitting.

Do be conscious of how you smell; just as at one extreme the smell of cigarette smoke and alcohol can be upsetting, paradoxically an overuse of chemical scents such as deodorant and aftershave can have an equally off-putting effect, even if you think that you smell fantastic! I am sure you are all sterling examples of cleanliness and hygiene, but occasionally we're all a bit prone to smelly feet – well worth hiding your shoes and changing your socks after work, to keep a pleasant and peaceful household.

Your partner's increased sense of smell is, in part, a natural protection against her inhaling or ingesting nasty toxins, which, via the placenta would end up in your baby's bloodstream. How tea or a fried egg fall into this category is a mystery, but their effect can be very real and is not something that you are going to want to promote.

'I Don't Like It'

Partially related to the increase in your partner's sense of smell and partly to do with subconscious fears concerning the baby's safety, will be your partner's sudden aversion to certain tastes, activities or even modes of transport.

Your partner will treat many activities differently and will sometimes seem to do things in extremes. For example, she may become very fond of walking and think nothing of walking six miles to the supermarket just for a bag of crisps, bypassing numerous shops on the way. Another day she may well be reluctant to walk anywhere and will quite happily wait for you to come home so that you can shop for her.

The partners of some of those interviewed went off their favourite television programmes; their favourite character's voice now grated on them, or the plot lines were suddenly exposed for the drivel they were. Some went off sex, as we have discussed, and some, it appeared, went off their husband! But of course, that was only temporary ... A father interviewed mentioned that, long before the physical act of driving became uncomfortable, his partner would refuse to drive. It wasn't that she was afraid to be in the car; it was the sudden fear that she might have an accident if driving or, although she was only twelve weeks pregnant and a long way off labour, a fear that her contractions might start.

To the onlooking father-to-be some of these decisions or actions can be unsettling and hard to understand. To your pregnant partner any fears, concerns or even dislikes are very real and very important. No matter how much she might have liked something before pregnancy, it is probably ruled out, until at least a few weeks after your baby is born. Expect Apathy, Antipathy and Antagonism, but in no fixed order and in varying degrees on different days. Tread carefully, my friend.

Hearts On Fire

Heartburn affects many women throughout their pregnancy, and the pain involved can be excruciating. Most of us have suffered from it once or twice after rushing a meal, but in pregnancy it often has nothing at all to do with eating. Rob learned long after his baby boy was born that many of the nocturnal visits to the bathroom his partner made were for a quick swig of Gaviscon, as much as a pit stop – although Claire admitted to combining the two events as much as possible. It was primarily intense indigestion and wind that woke her every hour, on the hour. Had Rob known, I am sure he would have suggested that she kept the bottle or tablets closer to the bed...

Heartburn is a common symptom of pregnancy. For the unfortunate it lasts throughout the pregnancy, but it is far more likely to become a regular visitor during the latter stages, due to the increased pressure that your baby is putting on your partner's stomach; thus, forcing stomach acid up the oesophagus. There is little your partner can do to eradicate or evade the symptoms. If it is going to happen then it is going to happen. Alkaline-based medicines such as indigestion tablets, and lots of them, are the only things that can help nullify the acidic burn.

'I Want, I Want!'

If ever you have thought that your partner shares any of the same character traits as Monica of *Friends*, you will very likely see these traits exaggerated over the coming months. Although you might regard your relationship as a fifty-fifty split; as your partner is now carrying and growing your baby all of the time, you are, whether you like it or not, going to be on 24-hour call for back rubs, cups of tea, fluffing of pillows, and all manner of other 'little' jobs until your baby is about eighteen and goes off to university. That's the division of labour, and you have absolutely no choice in the matter. Sorry.

Demands usually start off quite light, and are often voiced in an apologetic I wouldn't-normally-trouble-you sort of way. The months go by, the bulge gets bigger, and you just get hollered at, from the top of the stairs, to fetch this, that and the other. Not a please or thank you to be heard. Hold your tongue, smile, nod, and count your blessings that you don't have to give birth.

Expect to be thrown out of bed in the middle of the night because your body is too hot, too cold or making her itch. You will be required to clean your teeth three or four times a day to remove the 'stench' of garlic you ate last week. When you are asked to do something 'whenever you get a moment' that means RIGHT NOW, OR ELSE. It's all good preparation; young children are pretty demanding too.

Pregnancy can mean that you will have to become a bit of a

domestic goddess – this will probably not be your choice, but the routine jobs in the house will need to be done, and whether or not you are the sort of man who pulls his weight already, you will soon be well versed in the art of ironing, cleaning, washing and generally tidying up. I doubt that it is a conscious decision, but pregnant women get increasingly good at passing on the 'little jobs' as the pregnancy progresses. But then again, who said that they should be her jobs anyway?

Beware The Venom

There is no scorn like that of a woman. Or to be precise, a pregnant woman. Or, to be even more precise, the pregnant woman that you share a home, bed, and future with. Hormones, during pregnancy, will quickly become your worst enemy.

Hormones are the reason that so much happens as it should. They are the reason that your baby is developing in the womb, but they are also the reason that you will, on occasion, be completely ignored, shouted at, screamed at and generally abused. Welcome to the dark side of your partner. Just as a truth drug can determine if someone is guilty of doing something wrong, hormones flowing freely in your partner's body will cause the exposure of all your weaknesses and limitations, not to mention any misdemeanours committed six years ago before you even knew your partner. How could you not have guessed that all your partner wanted was a foot massage. Wasn't it obvious? Could you not feel it instinctively? Well, actually, no … I missed that one.

Your usually calm and collected partner can become, every now and again, hard work. This is the test of pregnancy for you, as a bloke. You love her, you love the fact that she is pregnant, and you love knowing that it was you who made her so. But did you expect such a Jekyll and Hyde performance. Probably not!

Over the course of the pregnancy and especially during labour you will be on the receiving end of a whole lot of pain and anger. Your partner has not had a personality transplant; it's the pregnancy talking, and therefore try to treat it like water off a duck's back. Some, if not all, of the words will hurt; you might occasionally wonder why you bothered coming home that evening, or even why you got her pregnant in the first place.

Thankfully, there is a flip-side. With all those hormones running around, your partner is also going to have a whole lot of love to express. And the fact is, despite the harsh words, that you are the most important person in the whole world to your partner right now. So look forward to many statements of complete and utter adoration and the occasional admission of dependence and total reliance. OK, the last two reactions might reflect a little conjecture on my behalf, but that's what our partners mean. Surely? We don't want to take all that abuse for nothing!

Expect and be prepared for the pregnancy venom. It really isn't your fault, or even hers. It is the hormones talking, despite the fact that your partner might be smiling wickedly while everything is said!

It's Got To Be You

Throughout this book one thing I'm striving to emphasize is that the keystone in your partner's support structure should be you, the partner. Yes, friends and family, doctors and midwives will also function as part of that support, but for the small day-to-day things that will help her get through the next months as smoothly as she can, it's got to be you.

If your partner has been pursuing a full-time career and likes to remain active, then pregnancy can be a real shock to her system – not just in terms of a baby growing in her womb, but also of how she spends her time on a daily basis. Certainly, in the latter stages of pregnancy, she will find herself unable to rush around and do all the things that she could before the pregnancy. But even before she goes on maternity leave, the slowing down in lifestyle can be a frustrating and boring business. She's tired and emotional, and she can't even uncork a bottle of wine to help her unwind, or go for a three-mile run. Although there's a lot to be excited about, she may find the waiting game infuriatingly slow.

You may find yourself coming home to the uninspiring sight of a sofa that bears the permanent imprint of your partner and on the floor (or perhaps the sink) evidence of some serious food consumption. Your partner will at times feel bored stiff. There are only so many TV soaps that any one person can take (about half an hour's worth), only so many pregnancy magazines published every month, and only so many times she can sit through your entire Netflix watchlist – even those Jackie Chan movies that were hitherto scorned at.

If she's suddenly stuck at home all day then you coming home from work will be comparable to Cleopatra sailing up (down?) the Nile on her burnished throne. So with a grand fanfare and all the pomp and circumstance one would expect from a saviour of sanity, you plonk yourself down on a chair, grumble a few words and relax in front of the box. Right? Wrong. Although you probably want nothing more than to unwind for half an hour yourself, sometimes you've got to bite the bullet, put it off until later, and allow your partner the chance to talk to an animate object for the first time that day. Dave at work, might be the most uninteresting person on the planet in your opinion, but you would even miss him if you didn't have anyone else to talk to.

The testing first trimester is a major trial of pregnancy. Although there are many more months to follow – and let's not forget the actual birth – this is the hardest psychologically. Use this phase, in between your panic attacks, as a valuable opportunity to enjoy each other's company. Use it to talk through issues relating to the pregnancy, from potential names to concerns about the upcoming weeks. Focus on each other and the relationship, before your partner gets too beleaguered with the pregnancy to do very much, or even think straight. The forthcoming arrival will be hugely time-consuming – enjoy your partner while you can. After all, you can probably relax a bit for the next three months
… can't you?

5. The 2nd Trimester

the second
trimester

... Or Who's The Daddy Now?

The second trimester, as experienced by blokes, is profound. It is a rite of passage that nobody prepares you for; it can also be your friend. Your partner will now be moving full throttle towards the birth. She will be between four and six months pregnant and you'll know about it. The physical evidence will be very much there for everyone, including you, to see.

Hand-in-hand with the growing bump may come a growing strain on your relationship. Your partner will be all hormonal; an untrained medical practitioner like you or me might imagine she is going mad. It is not unusual actually to feel slightly scared of your partner around this time (if not fear of her physical presence then at least of her temper, or of accidentally saying the wrong thing).

The unpredictability that started in the first trimester is growing daily. Even if you try to pussyfoot around, you will forget something or do something wrong, and learn about it in no uncertain terms. You no longer feel in control. As I mentioned before, one father described the experience of the second trimester as feeling like he had married his wife's sister or twin. So much is familiar – the voice, the hair, the nose – and yet so much is alien – the temper, the moods, and, on occasions, the language.

Despite being closer than ever before, both focused on the developing baby, in another respect you and your partner have never been further apart. She is going through an intense experience and you can only try to imagine how she feels. A person who you have always felt close to may now seem almost alien. Equally, she may not regard *you* in the same light as before, even though you feel that you have not changed or done anything to warrant this change of heart. You may suddenly feel that you don't gel together quite like you used to and it can be a very unsettling feeling.

Single No More

Through most of my interviews, the men said that the second trimester was when the realization of their new status really kicked in. The 'honeymoon period' and excitement of the first few months has worn off, the pregnancy is well established and everyone knows about it, and you suddenly start to ponder the big questions, like your purpose in life. Married or unmarried, before your partner became pregnant you were single. Single in the sense that the way you perceived yourself has probably not altered much since you were a teenager. The second trimester marks the important stage in which you suddenly regard yourself as a parent. For one man this happened when he went with his partner to the hospital for some antenatal tests. When the doctor asked for 'the mother's signature', he instinctively looked around for his mother. Then he realized that the doctor addressing his girlfriend, who he still saw as the foxy little rock chick he'd met in a seedy, smoky Amsterdam bar.

Married or not, your single days are well and truly over. Since you were a teenager a major instinct, focus, expense, cause of happiness and at times despair has been the concerted effort of chasing girls and women. Though you may have exchanged rings and vows with your partner, it is the coming baby that brings home the message, 'I am really settling down.'

The second trimester is often the time when our personal failings sail up to the forefront of our mind. We are beginning to think of the pregnancy in terms of an actual human baby, and with that comes the worry about what to say and do with our child and how that will affect their growth and development. In the short term we will need to get to grips with nappies and baths, to keep our child clean and healthy. In the longer term we know that we will probably be asked for help with homework, most likely on our least favourite subject. We have little or no experience of this responsibility and it is all the more frightening the closer we come to accepting it. Will I be a good dad, a mediocre dad or a bad dad? Will I cope? Will my relationship or marriage survive? Do I have the right skills for this challenge? Will I repeat the same mistakes as my father? Will I be better or worse at being a parent? Will my child resent me?

Fear Of Creating A Monster

Allied to this is the parallel thought of 'What exactly is going to emerge in a few months time?' Many fathers interviewed remembered that it was at some stage during the second trimester, just as they had gotten used to the whole 'having a baby' lark, that the real fear hit them. Never mind if the rest of the pregnancy and birth goes ahead without a hitch – what if we don't like what we get? Will my child be a bit weird looking? A boy instead of a girl? Have funny ears; Have a funny head; funny feet; a funny mouth? What about his or her temperament – is my child going to be the one causing carnage in the department store, much to the dismay of everyone looking on? Or will he have an uncontrollable temper that I am powerless to fight? Will my child be popular or the black sheep – what if he can't read and write, do simple maths or make friends? Will I like my child? Or worse, will my child like me?

The worries can go on *adnauseum*. Don't give yourself a hard time if you do become a worry wort. Pregnancy involves so many unknown factors that you would have to have a heart and head of steel not to experience some qualms. But most of those unknowns will turn out to the good – so relax and remember you will really help your partner and yourself by being as positive and optimistic about the pregnancy as possible.

It's Official

As I mentioned in the last chapter, although blood tests and the like may start early, your partner will often not have her official booking-in appointment until after the 12- week 'safe' period has passed. This is a sad reminder of the number of pregnancies that end in miscarriage before this time is up. It would be nice to say that after the first three months the pregnancy is home and dry and will definitely be without complications, but of course that's not always the case.

In the first trimester your partner was creating the placenta to protect and sustain your baby. During that time she may have felt too tired to continue with work, although various commitments often mean she had to. But that fatigue will subside somewhat during the magical second trimester. Once the placenta is completely formed, sustaining an ever-growing baby is actually plain sailing in com- parison. It is supposedly during this middle bit of the pregnancy that women start to really 'glow'. They are over the initial queasy first months and often now enjoy renewed vigour, making this is a good time to travel or do anything energetic.

Message In A Bottle

Your partner's urine will also be tested around now, mainly for protein and sugar. If either of these is found, it could indicate a problem. Too much sugar may indicate gestational diabetes, which will be further tested for by yet another blood test. Too much protein may indicate pre-eclampsia. The reason for the constant tests is to catch anything that could lead to a problem for your partner, or your baby, early on. Most conditions are treatable, and although your partner may argue differently, for the sake of a few tests it is always better to be safe than sorry.

Such will be your partner's familiarity with needles, that, by the time your baby is born, she may even be tempted to have a tattoo. (It has happened!) The hardest thing to bear is that once your baby is born, someone, somewhere, still wants to stick a needle or two into another member of your family – only now the target is your tiny baby; all necessary of course, but not pleasant for you or the baby!

Big Belly, Big Toes

There's no nice way to put this, unless you are quite partial to people metamorphosing in front of your very eyes. Over the forty (or thereabouts) weeks of pregnancy, no matter what size your partner was before the conception, by the time of the birth she will be significantly bigger; and not just her belly, mind you, but everything, right down to fingers, toes and, I would add, even eyebrows.

Weight gain is of course a natural 'effect' of pregnancy and something we expect to see, so long as it is happening to someone else other than our partner. When we witness physical changes in our beloved it is certainly never repulsive, in many cases far from it, but it does take us by surprise every now and again. Of course an advantage is that we will feel less guilty about our own protruding belly or love handles – by comparison they're nothing more than slight inconveniences.

Ironically, the whole first trimester is often spoiled a bit for us because we are impatient for the physical proof of pregnancy. Until we see the obvious growth, we are a little unsympathetic concerning many of the changes in our partners I listed earlier. Some fathers even admitted to forgetting that their partner was pregnant. Enter the second trimester and some of us are really wishing that they would change back to their old self again. Expect to see your partner grow outwards from every direction. The most noticeable changes, other than the belly, are her cheeks, fingers, ankles, feet, legs, bottom, breasts and arms (actually that doesn't leave an awful lot, does it.) Necks tend to stay pretty much the same, if that makes you feel any better.

A Full-Bodied Woman

For most women so-called 'morning sickness' eases up around the start of the second trimester. This means that she can eat considerably more, and the weight gain starts to show. Most annoying, particularly for the woman, is the stage before her bump really starts to become obvious and she simply looks a lot heavier than she would ordinarily. Rest assured that the weight gain is not permanent pounds acquired. Nor is it all food related. Without wishing to be insulting, pregnant women are like cacti; like their spiky, milky counterparts, they will be storing reserves at a level that far exceeds actual usage. It is the body's way of preparing for the worst – emergency provisions just in case. All that padding is your baby's protection and essential supplies, so most definitely something to be encouraged and applauded rather than criticized.

Many women have a hang-up about the weight they gain and will at some stage seek reassurance that it doesn't bother you. Let common sense prevail on this one. Anyway, most men genuinely find the woman carrying their baby utterly ravishing. Towards the end of your partner's pregnancy you may well be in awe of the size of her belly. It is likely to be enormous, and you, of course, will have the pictures to prove it. It will be absolutely solid to the touch and for a moment you wouldn't be wrong to think that she might actually burst. One father reported that his partner temporarily lost her belly button – she no longer had an 'inny' or an 'outy', it had simply merged with the skin over her belly. It is a short step from thinking, 'How will her stomach ever go back to normal,' to asking 'Exactly how big is my child going to be?'

Was That You?

If you thought that your partner was 'flatulence immaculate' then I am afraid that you were sorely wrong. One very common side effect of pregnancy is an increase in gas, from both ends. This will become increasingly obvious and amusing, at least for you. At first, your partner may wish to remain very ladylike and somewhat bashful of noises and smells escaping. After about three weeks of needless apologies, courteously placing a hand over her mouth and occasionally leaving the room, she will probably give up. The house will be filled with the joyous sounds of escaping gas, day and night, and you will no longer be told off for adding to the symphony yourself. Just make sure that you both get out of the habit once the baby is born.

The reason for the excess gas is mainly due to your partner's body keeping food in the stomach for a little longer than usual. Those of us that are not pregnant tend to waste as many nutrients as we use, with food rushing in one end and out the other. Because your partner is pregnant, her body is actually leeching off every molecule of sustenance, as if it might be the last morsel ever to pass her lips. The food sits in the gut longer, and like a fine Chianti begins to ferment. The gas has to come out and it chooses one of two ways to join the atmosphere.

Most men still find wind amusing, like the joke that never gets old or worn out. Your partner will have a much harder time than you will accepting that flatulence is going to be the norm for at least the rest of the pregnancy.

Stubborn Stools

Being constipated is incredibly uncomfortable. Imagine that feeling coupled with carrying a baby in your belly, and you come some way to understanding what your partner is going through. Uncomfortable, to say the least. Ironically, you have watched her eat more fibre and 'good poo foods' in the last week than you are likely to have consumed in the last year. But alas, there is stagnation, and no movements are forthcoming.

As with morning sickness, your partner may or may not suffer from constipation, and like morning sickness it will come in waves. Most likely it will not be discussed, but you will get the sneaking suspicion that something is afoot about the time that you too need to sit on the daily throne, and it remains engaged for a far longer time than even you would dare read the paper for.

A generous helping of bran or muesli may not be the most appetizing way to start the day, but it might help with those stubborn stools!

Taking The Strain

Stubborn stools can go on to cause haemorrhoids, for some strange reason otherwise known as piles. Before I had them, I thought that haemorrhoids were funny things that happened to old people, but they are not funny in the slightest (except when Nobby Piles has them in Viz). I have had piles on two occasions and I still carry the emotional scars to this day.

The squeamish among you can cross your legs now – having piles is like having tiny shards of glass, or a nicked razor blade, inserted into the skin around your anus. There's really no nicer way of explaining it. The pain, sometimes, is quite bearable, and you might even forget about it, unless of course you have to sit down or wipe your bum too fast after a poo – both activities will bring tears to the eyes of a grown man within seconds, and sadly, you generally have to do one or the other at least once a day.

Piles are yet another little bugbear in the life of the pregnant woman. Not all will get them, but many do. During pregnancy, piles can be caused either by straining too much while having a poo or by the general weight of the baby bearing down on the internal organs. Often piles are avoided the whole way through pregnancy, only to make a cheeky appearance during the birth. As many women equate the pushing feeling related to giving birth to that of expelling a rather stubborn stool, it is almost inevitable that the huge effort of giving birth is going to leave one or two side effects, none of which are likely to come close to the pain and discomfort of haemorrhoids, save maybe an episiotomy.

Some fathers interviewed admitted that when their partner was further on in the pregnancy they were promoted to chief applicator of a generous dose of Anusol on the target area, at their partner's request. Not quite what they had in mind when they imagined playing with their partner's bottom that night, but very much part of the contract that they signed up for when their marriage vows included 'in sickness and in health'.

Waterworks

As the baby grows, so does the pressure on your partner's bladder, which, prior to pregnancy was second only to the stomach in the fight for room. Now junior has put in an appearance, all of her organs have to shift around and give in to the demands of the now mighty uterus. Probably by now your partner's increased need to wee is keeping you both up at night with an almost hourly visit to the bathroom. As pregnancy progresses, and certainly around the

eight-month mark, your partner may even suffer from a bit of leakage – officially known as stress incontinence. Although this does not mean that she will wet herself every day, a violent sneeze, cough or jolt can cause her to leak. Another good reason to remind her to keep up with the pelvic-floor exercises – not that she's likely to be in the mood to hear this if she's just embarrassed herself again.

Turning On The Waterworks

There is a good possibility that your partner will become a complete bundle of tears during the months of pregnancy
– even the most hardened of women can go weak at the knees and start crying uncontrollably at the sight of babies or small children. This phenomenon manifests itself most frequently when watching television. The drug of the nation, with its cathode-ray nipple, may well wean your partner through the latter stages of pregnancy and maternity leave whether you like it or not. The tears may be sparked off while you are watching the most innocuous news clip or documentary. Maybe something completely unrelated to children or babies – cute bunnies in a field, or three-for-two offers at Iceland, for example.

Fathers interviewed mentioned numerous experiences; the most common occurrence of spontaneous tears was during adverts for nappies or baby shampoo. Once the crying starts, you'll get used to it, although at first it can be quite alarming. When questioned, your partner may be unable to explain why she felt the need to cry. It seems to her to be a combination of happiness, sadness, worry and excitement; the realisation that one day she will be playing with her own child in a bath, or washing his or her hair, or looking on as the child dances around the room dressed only in a nappy. Several honest fathers even admitted they'd been subject to the odd sniffle themselves.

Deeply Dizzy

Many women find themselves fainting for the first time in pregnancy. Dizziness will come and go, and may be triggered by the season, the use of excessive central heating or by simply standing up too fast. Fainting is less common, but with so much more area to pump blood round, your partner's body can become pushed. Any sudden movement takes its toll, causing a sudden drop in blood pressure, and usually the body follows suit; right back down onto the sofa.

Your partner will quickly learn to get up more slowly and generally not rush around so much, but it is nice to know in advance that her eyes rolling around in their sockets are not disapproval at your lightning wit, merely a spot of dizziness.

Gasp And Wheeze

Another change during the second trimester is your partner's breathing. As the baby gets bigger the diaphragm is forced up. This is to help rearrange the internal organs, which had become quite used to their allotted place within her body. The baby will take what space it can, which means denying the lungs of some of their rightful domain.

The net effect is that your partner may find herself short of breath throughout the day. The simplest of tasks become harder. Combined with a sore back caused by the weight of the baby, bad posture, swollen feet, a slow and awkward walk, and general fatigue, you could be forgiven for thinking that your partner has seen better times. Pregnancy really is a whole-body experience for her, whereas it's just something that plays on your mind and might mean you have to do a fair bit around the house.

Payback Time

There might well be competition in the bedroom from the start of the second trimester. Your partner's nose may become blocked during the pregnancy leading to snoring and, on occasion, aponea, which is short periods when she stops breathing. Not pleasant to listen to, and if the pillows have already made an appearance in the bed, together with the frequent trips to the loo, you may well be considering hoofing the dog out of his kennel and sleeping down there. It's progesterone playing havoc again and will most probably stop once the baby is born. The way to minimize snoring is to do what she's been telling *you* to do for goodness knows how long: sleep on your side and avoid the booze and fags. These last two are unlikely to be an issue during pregnancy and she'll most probably be sleeping on her side anyway, to help relieve the pressure of the baby – so if the snoring continues it looks like you're stuck with it for the next few months.

Where Am I, Who Am I?

Your partner may well become incredibly scatty during the pregnancy. In fact, the further on in the pregnancy she is, the more it becomes evident. Suddenly, those all-important appointments, (quite possibly the only appointment she has that week) will slip her mind. It is the only real reason that she will need to leave the house this month – but she forgets. I found it funny and I hope that you do too. No matter how many sticky notes she might leave for herself around the house, about the time that she should be on her way, Jill will pop round for a chat, or she will have an insatiable urge to buy something for the baby. Doctors and midwives must bear the brunt of this, as it is probably their appointment that has been missed. Generally, I think they are quite understanding and don't mind rescheduling too much.

Forgetfulness and lack of focus seem to go hand in hand. Mistakes might well happen at work and your partner's angora sweater might accidentally end up in the tumble dryer. Becoming scatty is an understandable by-product of pregnancy, and tends to do no one any harm. In a way, it makes the whole experience more endearing.

The second trimester brings with it its own challenges, but do enjoy what, in relative terms, is a bit of an easy ride. It will only get more intense from here on in and time will really start to fly. Long-haul flights may be both out of the question and out of budget, but this really is your last chance for the foreseeable future for a short break somewhere (anywhere!). Hopefully the DIY is well underway and your home is being transformed into a veritable baby playground. The more advanced among you will even be down on hands and knees making sure that everything is toddler-proof. The countdown is about to begin as we welcome the third trimester into our lives.

6. The 3rd Trimester

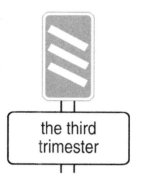

the third
trimester

... Or How It All Clicks Into Place

Nearing the home straight, you are probably even starting to feel a little bit excited about soon becoming a dad. You are starting to see there may be more benefits to this than just having someone to fetch the remote from the other side of the room.

The third trimester, covering months seven to nine of the pregnancy, is probably most profound for your partner. She is going to become almost completely incapacitated by the baby inside her. It is affecting her breathing, weeing, sleeping, appetite, energy and concentration; and that's just the tip of the iceberg.

The third trimester marks the beginning of the end in this journey of pregnancy, and although you will not have the same freedom as you might have enjoyed earlier, tempers will by and large be more controlled. The house will be either nearly, or completely, finished, in anticipation of the new arrival. There will be various pieces of baby hardware in the kitchen, in the cupboard and maybe in the attic. This is as real as it has ever felt, and as if you needed another reminder, your partner's belly is getting really, really big.

Other than your baby's growth, everything else slows down a notch in the third trimester. Your partner does, quite literally; and you do, too, in terms of racing emotions and worries. This is the lull before the storm, and no matter how perfect a storm it might be, it's still a storm.

So Tired!

In the last few months your partner will be feeling exhausted for many reasons – partly due to lack of sleep and partly just to the physical effort of carrying the baby and continuing to feed and grow it.

Obviously, she should try and rest more; easy if she is a lady that lunches, but not so easy if she is either working or looking after other children, or both! If you are not familiar with the domestic appliances, or domestic tasks that need to be done on a regular basis, it will be a baptism of fire. There's dinner to be cooked, hoovering and cleaning to be done, and if you work in an office, at least five shirts to be ironed every week.

There is one school of thought that says you should encourage your partner to take at least some exercise, even if she complains of fatigue. In the same way that if you eat too much in the evening you will be ravenous in the morning, so the body gets used to the new levels of food during pregnancy and expects the same. And leading a sedentary existence adds to the fatigue, as every movement becomes more exhausting still. You will know (and more accurately your partner will know) what her limitations are.

Although she won't be running any marathons, a quick walk to the shops is a great idea. Yoga is a particularly good form of exercise too and there are many antenatal yoga classes around. As well as helping her with breathing and posture she'll meet women at the same stage of pregnancy and lots of potential new friends.

But most of the time she's going to be parked on the sofa. By the time your baby reaches the age of two, you will probably need a new couch. Most of the damage will be from regurgitated milk, yoghurt, jam and chocolate stains; but you knew it needed replacing anyway at the time of birth because your partner left such a big imprint of herself during pregnancy that it makes anyone sitting on the sofa feel like they are at a strange angle – which they are. Tiredness: it doesn't just kill on the roads, it kills in the pocket too.

The Joy Of ... Sleep

Ahh! The joy of an undisturbed full night of sleep – those were the days! Although it is your partner who will be waking up to go to the loo a couple of times every night, unless you really are a heavy sleeper, or you sleep in a different room, you will probably be awake along with her. As beautiful as they are, heavily pregnant women are not the most delicate of creatures and getting in and out of bed becomes a major operation, which may even require your assistance. Expect to become very familiar with the wee small hours of the morning over the coming months.

During the later stages of your partner's pregnancy it will be actually quite amazing if you are still able to fit into the bed. Every night your partner may create a nest for herself, amazing to behold yet impossible to share comfortably. Do not be surprised if at one stage there are about ten pillows in the bed, all at rather obtuse angles, that leave you just about enough room (circa six inches by eight inches) to fit in somewhere, as long as you lay on your side and do not move an inch. The pillows will be arranged to make your partner as comfortable as possible – one behind her back, two between her legs, one underneath the bump and so on. This means that going to the loo is actually a logistical nightmare. The process of getting out of the bed becomes even more difficult and slow, and when nature's call has been answered, on comes the light and it's time for the pillows to be placed back into position. If you are brave you might want to suggest a colostomy bag or catheter be fitted, but you won't mean it.

Many women see the process of getting up a few times a night during pregnancy as the body's way of preparing her to cope with night-time feeds after the birth. So in a way it is also preparation for you too. It may be many years before you can once again rest assured that you will have a full, undisturbed night's sleep, with just the two of you in the bed. I still await that day.

Chris complained that his wife would not only build a nest and hog the covers, she would also insist on the window being left open wide to the elements. Cocooned in a huge double duvet and immersed in the feather and down of numerous pillows, she did not feel the cold November chill. Sadly the soon-to-be father did, and as any attempt to reclaim said covers resulted in an earbashing of gargantuan proportions, he would promptly take himself off to the comforts of his sleeping bag on the lounge floor.

Earth Mother

Your partner will want to set up the perfect environment for the new baby. This is related to nesting, but is about more than just cleanliness and tidiness. We are talking about having the right smells in the house, the right fabric on the sofa, the right chairs and the right curtains, and it all has to look just right.

Do not be surprised if your partner has a sudden interest in home baking (in fact enjoy it; she will probably cook way too many cookies and it would be a shame to throw them away!). Baking, cooking and a strange fascination with pelmets are your partner's way of becoming more 'motherly'. Although you might strongly dislike the new floral pattern that appears to dominate the lounge, you're not going to turn your nose up at cakes fresh out of the oven. There might, unfortunately, be some new house rules enforced – probably relating to where you currently leave your dirty laundry, wet towels and various shoes. What your partner is after is a cleaner, tidier, nicer-looking home

– and the main culprit for all these years is probably you.

Earth Calling Mother ...

It might be four in the morning, but that seems a perfectly logical time for your partner to awaken, don her overalls, and start painting the nursery walls in a rather fetching shade of lime green. Of course, it might be just her way of showing her complete contempt for your empty promises over the last six months that you were going to get round to doing the job yourself. But you didn't, did you? There was always something else more important to do first, and now you will feel guilt like never before.

Odd behaviour is commonplace during pregnancy and may manifest in various ways, from the slightly daft to the downright dangerous. Zazz, a father interviewed, described how he came home from work to catch his wife balancing on tiptoes on top of a chair, which in turn was placed on a coffee table, which was at the top of a very steep set of stairs. She was changing a light bulb at eight months into the pregnancy and was literally risking life, limb, and, in her husband's opinion, their unborn baby, for the sake of not waiting twenty minutes for him to get home. Her counter- argument involved some choice language and a gentle reminder that she had been asking him to change that bulb for nearly two weeks. He hadn't done it, but suddenly he desperately wished he had.

Between the cleaning, the crying, the wacky sleep pattern and the behavioural shift, the feeling of having married your partner's twin sister changes from a humorous notion to a real possibility.

Nesting – It's Not Just For The Birds!

Although commonly attributed to pregnant women I think that all men also 'nest' in one way or another. Nesting is a way of preparing your home for the new baby. For women it often means an intense cleaning of the house, for you it might be washing the car or putting a new sub-woofer in the boot. I was completely unaware of the phenomenon until Lisa noticed that I had spent the past few days sorting out books on a bookshelf, going through old papers and binning unnecessary junk. To cap it all off I made a very generous donation of old clothes, CDs and books to the local charity shops. Although we had bought a number of items for Alia, it was not as if we were desperate for space, so I can only assume that deep down I was preparing the house for the new arrival. I must confess that it was a particularly liberating experience chucking out useless photos and paraphernalia from school that I had been carrying from house to house for nearly 15 years.

Another Quiet Night In?

As the pregnancy progresses, so will your partner's discomfort. There are the obvious physical restrictions that the baby is placing on her internal organs, which make even sitting down if not painful then certainly unpleasant. This effectively rules out many activities that you might ordinarily enjoy as a couple, such as going to the cinema and theatre.

She may also feel disinclined to sit in smoky bars and restaurants; let's face it, if you had to sit and listen to Dave's drunken ramblings for hours on end without the hazy filter of cigarettes or alcohol, you'd probably rather stay at home too. This will probably impact your social life, especially towards the latter stages of the pregnancy. Some fathers did the honourable thing and spent a lot more time at home, suffering alongside their partner. Most of us, myself included, expressed our disappointment at having to go out with the lads without our partners, but promptly went off for the night regardless.

Maybe you needn't feel too guilty about this. Mark's wife positively encouraged him to get down to the pub so that she could have the house to herself. She much preferred to be able to weep uninhibitedly at the soppy baby programmes, or simply fixate goggle-eyed on whatever junk TV happened to be on, without his disapproving cynicism cramping her style.

Talk To The Bump, 'Cause The Ears Are Listening

At some point in this final trimester your partner will most definitely be showing, and this means it's time to talk to the bump. Embarrassing as it may sound – and embarrassing it is, especially to begin with – it will begin the bond between you and your baby.

Some fathers interviewed said that their unborn child would recognize their voice and kick frantically when they heard it during the latter months of pregnancy. The baby responding to familiar voices is common and an important ego-booster for the dad-to-be. Part of the helplessness that fathers feel during pregnancy is down to the feeling that they can't really do anything for the baby. Bump conversations are a good place to start – for you, your baby and your partner. Fifteen minutes an evening, either on a sofa or in bed, can become a very relaxing and intimate time for the three of you (or four, or five, if you're expecting more).

During the latter stages of the pregnancy it might be a good idea to test potential names out on the bump. If your baby kicks you could take that as a sign of approval. A word of warning: whenever you are asked if you would like to feel baby kicking, more often than not as soon as you reach over to feel the bump, your baby will stop kicking. As if playing a cruel game he or she will suddenly decide to fall asleep the moment you are invited to feel a kick or a punch. But when baby does play, being able to feel and on occasions see your baby kicking from within the womb is fantastic. For some men it can become a little boring, but that will be almost impossible to say to your partner; she is acutely conscious of every one of those little kicks and punches.

If Music Be The Food Of Love ...

Music is good for both you and your partner and of course your baby. Definitive tests have shown that if babies are played the same piece of music over and over again throughout the pregnancy, they respond to it immediately on hearing it after the birth, no matter how tiny they are. Amazing really. If either of you are talented enough to play an instrument, pregnancy is the time to dust off the scores, wipe down the piano and play on. Us layabouts will have to rely on pre-recorded efforts for our fix.

I began to feel a real bond with the unborn Alia when she would react to CDs being played in the car (my car, my music!). Her reaction was to kick and punch violently, as if Lisa's belly was a 3D graphic equalizer. She loved Asian Sitar and Kung Fu film soundtracks. Gangsta' rap and drum and bass were firm favourites. Try her on a bit of pop or classical and she'd stop. Radio 4 was a no-no, and Radio 1 not much better. My girl had taste and was not afraid to show it. With hindsight she might have been kicking and punching to make the racket stop, but I like to believe she liked it. The proof is always in the pudding, but we found once Alia had gone past the sleep-as-soon-as-you-drive- anywhere-in-the-car stage, if we felt she needed a sleep we would play a tune that had been common fare during the pregnancy. She immediately recognized the tune, smiled briefly, and was away with the fairies within seconds. Try it and see for yourself.

Antenatal Groups

It's during the third trimester that you're most likely to be dragged (sorry, I mean asked to go) to some antenatal classes. These are usually run by your partner's local health authority, hospital or group practice, and will be close to where you live. If you and your partner live in the UK, you can also join the National Childbirth Trust, which is a subscription-based service for people planning, expecting, or with children. Your partner may want to go to both the NHS classes and the NCT-run sessions; and that probably means that you are going too, whether you like it or not.

It seems that most men have a love-hate relationship with

these groups. They protested loudly that they hated going, but secretly they loved the rich source of amusing anecdotes they provided. Every man loves a good NCT story and most who attended will have one. My view is that if you miss out on these, you're missing out on a major aspect of the pregnancy – and not just in terms of what you might learn.

However, the bottom line is that the classes are run to give you and your partner an insight into what to expect before, during and after labour. They'll probably be a mixture of secondary school biology, first aid, and home economics. In a nutshell, I found the few NCT classes that I attended a bit fluffy (throw a ball, and shout out the name of the person you are throwing it to) and the NHS classes pretty intense (video of actual vaginal birth, on big screen, 20 minutes after wolfing down my dinner).

NCT

I'm going to start off by saying that I remain a committed and fully paid-up member of the NCT (National Childbirth Trust). The NCT is a well-established, well-run organization that offers a fantastic support network for all pregnant women and new mothers. But this book is all about personal accounts and therefore I will reveal that I did not get on too well with the antenatal groups I went to. In general, I know that they provide an important service and, as a whole, they shouldn't be knocked, but they really weren't for me. I found the classes were sometimes a bit patronizing to the men and I even got the impression that perhaps we were only invited along so that our partners had the opportunity to show us off physically; though why they would want to do that after a day in the office and a fair old commute is beyond me.

With the group I attended, whenever the organizer, probably a practising or retired midwife, would direct a question at the men, there was an uncomfortable silence mixed with a bit of grumbling and the occasional loud whisper from one of the pregnant women to her partner: 'Go on, you know this.' Eventually the question would be reluctantly answered and the class would move on, a terribly slow and laborious process to say the least.

No one wanted to seem to be the swot and no one wanted to admit that they hadn't been reading the books that their partners had been collecting over the previous six months. Ironically, the question on most people's minds, which is never mentioned at these sort of things; is 'I'm s****ing myself about this whole thing. Does anyone else feel the same way?' Instead we hold our tongues, sniff other people's feet and look at the floor. I probably neglected to mention the fact that I got into a bit of a row with the organizer on my first session, which did stain my opinion a bit. Not only did she assume that I had milk in my coffee, but there was a severe, and very obvious, lack of custard creams on offer. Then she asked if anyone had had gas and air. After a painful silence that had me nearly turning on her television, I volunteered that I had, on a couple of occasions. The organizer asked me to explain to the group what it was like to take, and the effects you were likely to experience, which I did – and she said that I was incorrect. The cheek! Seriously though, most of the other couples who attended the classes both enjoyed and appreciated the sessions. Certainly your partner will not have anxieties (or hang-ups?) about antenatal classes and will invariably get a lot of invaluable information out of them. More importantly, she is likely to make a number of lasting friendships from any groups that she attends, and these friendships often last for years and years, as your respective children all grow up and go through the same phases and hurdles at the same time. When you are on your own in a house for weeks on end with only a helpless baby for company, it is those friendships that will help pass the time and allay any fears you might have.

It's One Way Of Making Friends ...

Personally, I would really like to have met the other fathers in our group outside the class setting, say in a pub for a pint. I'm sure we would have all got on very well, although I accept that no one would have breathed a word about pregnancy or birth – it would all have been office talk and football. Instead we all sat (or lay) patiently at our partner's sides, feeling terribly awkward and not at all at ease.

Max, a self-confessed anti-tree-hugger, initially told his wife Suzie that there was no way he was going to attend anything that might involve 'standing in a circle, breathing together and holding hands'. After the first two meetings, tired of being the only 'single parent', she pleaded with him to go with her. Reassured that there was nothing 'heeby-jeeby' about it at all, Max reluctantly agreed. However, when he turned up Suzie noticed he was slightly the worse for wear. But things didn't go too badly until the end of the session when they all lay down quietly in 'corpse pose' in the darkened room, to relax to some Maori meditation music. Drifting over from Max's corner came the unmistakable sound of drunken snoring.

In the group that I attended, at one stage we did an exercise that involved us sitting on the carpet, back-to-back with our partners. The organizer dimmed her lights and lit some candles. We tried to breathe in unison, but I was more concerned with an itch I got on my hand after touching the carpet. Perhaps I'm shallow but for me it wasn't relaxing or useful, just daft. Going that close to about twenty sets of sweaty socks is not my idea of relaxation on a Wednesday night, especially when there was Liverpool playing in the Champions League as a very valid alternative.

In Malcolm's class, there was a definite divide of interests when a video played showing women breastfeeding. The pregnant women smiled, saying 'Ohh' and 'Ahh'. Similar sounds were emitted from the men in the room, but whereas their partners were looking forward to the day they too could feed a new-born, their other halves were simply admiring the breasts.

It's All About Networking

Once you have convinced yourself that organizations such as the NCT in the UK and in USA are not 'Freemasonry For Women', you will begin to see the huge benefits that any organization supporting pregnant women offers. Whenever we do anything new, we like to talk to people who have had similar experiences. Through the group chats, your partner will be empowered to make decisions knowing the full facts. There is a no-holds-barred approach to telling the truth about how good a particular hospital is, or how the pain relief will really affect her. Once your baby is born, your partner may well continue to meet up with the other new mums; they swap and sell clothes, (saving you and your partner a fortune) and establish a community of mothers, which is both healthy and emotionally good for your partner.

So it might mean that Doris will pop round a bit too much, to eat your biscuits and drink your coffee, but this is networking, and new mums can be incredibly lonely and anxious in those first weeks after the birth. And while you're fighting with other commuters on the M1, hating your job and your boss, remember that your partner would yearn for a chance to have an hour sitting in traffic, on her own, without a child attached to her breast like a limpet. Instead, Doris and friends give her that much needed break, just by being there.

The Stiff Upper Lip Syndrome

No matter how much you try to make an honest go of it, your experience of the antenatal classes is going to be very different from your partner's. Maybe it stems from us blokes' general unwillingness to talk about emotions, or our partner's bits, in front of, or to, other people. I would like to think that in our own little way we are loyal and true to our partners. Our silence, therefore, is not an act of defiance or disinterest, but of protection. Not sure if that would hold up in a court of law, but it's what some of us think.

However, in the two sessions I attended I did learn quite a lot about the pain relief available during labour. Childish as I am, I found it quite bizarre to hear a middle- aged auntie-type talking to me about opiate-based drugs, and their application, without adding that I was in fact being arrested for something concerning said application.

No Pain, No Gain!

Sadly, there seems to be a certain amount of moral judgement attached to the use of pain-killers during labour. One father attended an antenatal day at a centre that advocated 'natural' childbirth. There he met quite a few people of both sexes who implied that your partner accepting anything other than unbearable pain is a complete and utter cop out. Amazingly, there seemed to be a ranking system relating to the level of assistance that was used to assist a birth.

'It's cool to have your baby without drug assistance.' 'Yes, I
even refused the gas and air. I wanted to really
feel my child coming out.'

'Oh, epidural; that's the slacker's option. That must have
made things easier.'

Yes, of course it did. Isn't that the whole point! Personally, if
I had endured 17 hours of incredible pain already, I would have
opted for absolutely anything available, whether that came in capsule
or intravenous form, and lapped every single milligram up!

And While We're On The Subject ...

The kind of pain relief your partner opts for is very much her
decision. Keep private your thoughts on her plan to rely only on
lavender aromatherapy candles and a few drops of Rescue Remedy.
However, it is wise to be clued up about the more common forms
on offer, and to discuss them with her in plenty of time, as you may
be the only one capable of conveying her real wishes at the critical
hour.

TENS Machine

Starting with the mildest first, TENS stands for Transcutaneous
Electrical Nerve Stimulation. It is not dissimilar to those
machines people get to stimulate their abdominal muscles so that
they can eat a couple of burgers and do the equivalent of 2,000 sit-
ups without having to miss the *Baywatch* omnibus. The battery-
powered box is attached to your partner's belt and you or the
midwife will place the sticky pads strategically on her back. By

pressing the button, small electrical charges are sent into the wearer's back causing a massage-like effect.

Essentially the TENS machine allows the user to mass- produce endorphins which are useful in helping to counteract the pain of contractions. It is important that the TENS machine is put to work very early on in the labour, otherwise it will be useless. Ideally your partner will start off with the machine at its lowest setting. As the pain of contractions increases, so does the setting of the TENS machine. Many people from the 'natural' birth camp believe strongly in the use of TENS machines. The advantage of using TENS is that your partner controls the settings, and feeling in control is of paramount importance during labour; plus it does not affect your baby in any way and can be used for as long as your partner wants without any side effects.

There are mixed views on their actual effectiveness and a fair few have been thrown at a wall in frustration. The use of TENS machines mainly benefits during the early stages of labour, especially when labour starts at home and there are a few hours to go before you have to go to hospital. There will come a point when the contractions are so strong that the wires are actually a hindrance and inconvenience, more than a help. Once the midwife wants to monitor your baby's heart rate then the TENS machine may have to be disconnected anyway.

You will need to hire a TENS machine if that is the route that you and your partner want to follow. They are relatively inexpensive and widely available. There are a few sources listed in Chapter Twelve. Alternatively you could recommend a couple of paracetamol and a feather duster ...

Gas And Air (Entonox)

Gas and air, formally known as Entonox, is a gas made up of 50 per cent nitrous oxide and 50 per cent oxygen. In the hospital it is usually available through a pipe from the wall, and in home births it is administered through a mask attached to a small cylinder. It is actually odourless, but many people mistake the smell of the plastic or rubber mask as the smell of the gas.

Even those in the natural camp will usually have a breath or two of gas and air, and certainly in the early stages of labour it takes the bite off the contractions. If required, it can be used throughout the labour. It is self- administered by breathing in as the contractions peak. Not dissimilar to SCUBA apparatus the two-way valve allows the mixture to be inhaled, whilst carbon dioxide is expelled. Within a few seconds, you will feel perfectly normal again. And she might feel better too.

In fairness to Entonox, its appeal is in its simplicity and in your partner being able to control the dosage and frequency. After a matter of seconds, the effects wear off, allowing your partner to feel fully in control. Also, the added advantage of the deep breaths and the oxygen content will only help your baby in what can be a very stressful time for her or him as much as your partner.

On the flip-side of the coin, you get what you pay for, and gas and air does have its limitations with regard to actual effectiveness. As labour progresses so will your partner's irritability. Combined with the baby's heart-monitor wires, the gas and air mask or mouthpiece can simply confuse your partner and start to get in the way. Many fathers whose partners used gas and air also saw the mask being chucked across the room, following the same sad fate at the TENS machine. If you were to compare it to alcohol it would be like opting for the half-a-lager-shandy rather than the entire bottle of Smirnoff.

Pethidine

Some fathers gave a bit too much away about their younger (or in some circumstances their current) lifestyles when asked to describe the effect that Pethidine had had on their partners. It is a very powerful drug and although the effects last a matter of hours for your partner, it will affect your baby for a number of days after birth.

Pethidine is a synthetic version of morphine. Heralded as a wonder drug in the 1940s it is still widely used today, although many doctors favour giving an epidural, which has more of a local anaesthetic effect, rather than causing the general numbness you get with pethidine. Administered via an injection, most likely in your partner's bottom, it is often used in conjunction with another drug to combat any sickness she might feel.

Pethidine will not be administered if your partner is too close to giving birth, because of the effects it will have on your baby and also because it might slow down the labour. The main benefits of pethidine are that it will relax your partner and simply help her to cope. The effects are euphoria coupled with intense drowsiness. For a very long labour it can be ideal as a 'break' from the pain and the effort, and sometimes it will have worn off just sufficiently for your partner to enjoy birth. In its favour, the drug can be administered in varying doses by the midwife, which allows a quick turnaround from decision to implementation
– at a time when you and your partner are more conscious of time passing than possibly during any other experience in life. Pethidine is even a viable option for home birth and eases a lot of worries for pregnant women and their blokes, in that they can have the comforts of medical science right there in their comfortable home.

Pethidine has been blamed for having such a strong effect

on some women that they have actually slept through the pregnancy (some of us blokes would be applauding if it was us giving birth)! The most important thing to take into account is that the drug will pass through the placenta into your baby's bloodstream. It is likely that if your partner has pethidine then the baby will be very sleepy for a few days after birth and is unlikely to feed well.

Epidural

This is the daddy of pain relief. No longer will you wince at getting a holiday jab in the backside after you have seen one of these bad boys administered.

The epidural is actually the area in the small of the back into which the local anaesthetic is injected, using a curved, hollow needle. A tube is inserted into the hollow of the needle and the needle is removed, essentially leaving a pipe through which the local anaesthetic is fed. The tube will be taped to your partner's back and over her shoulder. The anaesthetist injects a local anaesthetic (similar to what you would have at the dentist) into the tube to numb the lower part of her abdomen. Most likely, her legs and feet will go numb as well. The benefit of an epidural is that it stops the pain of contractions and childbirth whilst allowing the woman to feel fully conscious. Unlike pethidine it does not affect the brain, allowing your partner, although numb, to be a little more in control of the situation. The dosage will either be controlled by a primed pump or by your partner. Even the most steadfast from the natural camp have buckled (understandably) after 19 hours of excruciating pain and begged for the 'Full Monty' to help them through to the birth. The midwife will have the final say on the matter, but will generally only refuse to administer it if your partner is very close to giving birth. A successful epidural relies heavily on a skilled anaesthetist. On occasions only one side of the body is anaesthetized, which is not only frustrating but does little to help the pain.

Your partner will not be able to move around or change position as often, or as drastically, once the epidural has been administered, but the need for this should be dramatically reduced. The use of an epidural will also mean that your partner will be hooked up with a drip to ensure that her blood pressure remains at a safe level, for the benefit of her and, equally importantly, your baby. A catheter will generally also be applied to assist the now numb bladder function.

Another common complaint is that having an epidural can lessen the control the mother has over the birth. If she can't feel the contractions at all, she has to rely on the doctor and midwife telling her when to push. There is some evidence that suggests labour is longer for this reason.

The Hospital Tour

If your partner has opted for a hospital birth, the highlight in your calendar should be the obligatory visit to the maternity ward. This is a useful exercise simply because you have never needed to be in one before. A pre-visit and sighting of all the equipment can temper the most nervous of fathers, or instil absolute fear into the most blasé. Often arranged by the antenatal class, first-time mums (and dads) are encouraged to visit the maternity ward of the hospital where the delivery is to take place. Quite simply it is so that you both know where you're supposed to go when her waters break on the Saturday morning shop at Sainsbury's; and also to help minimize any dread or fear you might have of what goes on behind the closed doors. Except, of course, that the doors behind which there is any action going on are closed during the pre-visit, so the whole thing might seem a little sterile.

A Room Of Your Own

All hospitals differ. Wards will be of different sizes; some able to hold up to twenty women and new-born babies, some with a more private four-to-a-room setting. You may, depending on the facilities in your hospital, be able to book a private room. It is important that this is done when you first book in (once labour begins, not on this visit!). It will cost you, but probably less than £100 in the UK, which, given how much you have already spent on baby stuff is merely a drop in the ocean – and the benefits will be huge. The maternity ward, no matter how big or small, is a pretty public place. You only need to bear in mind that you lot are walking around for a start, and your group may not be the only tour organized for that day. Further, the inclusion of curtains for each 'cubicle' is of limited value, because they never quite close properly and they certainly don't block sound.

You At The Back, Pay Attention!

The tour is usually very upbeat and will be most people's first chance to see the inside of a delivery suite, a water-birth pool, and all the various instruments that may or may not be necessary to assist in the birth of your child. A few dads ask for a quick go on the gas and air, but usually receive a stern look for their efforts. Don't worry; it's much easier to steal a few gulps of the stuff when the real thing comes round. Although still very clinical, the maternity ward is by far the most pleasant area in a hospital, but you can't help but notice the smell of disinfectant that tends to haunt these places.

You are unlikely before this to have seen so many women, in various stages of their confinement, in such great numbers and so close together. Imagine ten or so penguins racing each other to get to the juicy fish that has just been tossed into the enclosure. Like a gaggle of geese, the women tend to form a pack, using strength in numbers; it's lucky that there are huge reinforced swinging doors in hospitals because, like a very angry rugby team, when the gang starts moving, things should get out of the way.

Most women find the pre-visit experience very useful and soak up as much as they can in what can only be about 20 minutes. They ask pertinent questions and observe everything. The blokes, however, tend to stand around feeling a bit daft, fiddling with their pockets and looking at the pattern on the floor. I found the whole thing a little reminiscent of walking down a school corridor to the headmaster's office.

And Finally....

These last few weeks might be a good time to try and gen up a bit about what happens after the baby is born; as you get closer and closer to D-day, you're going to become too preoccupied with the birth to think about anything else. I've put down a few practical tips in Chapter 11, for starters.

You've come a long way since the moment you found out that your partner was expecting, and whilst the whole process may or may not have been a wholly enjoyable experience, it has certainly been an eye-opener. You've learnt a lot more about yourself and your partner, and I am sure that having been through the ups and downs you can't think of a single other person you would prefer to have a baby with. No matter how hard it has all seemed, someone, somewhere had it worse – a lot worse, according to some of the accounts I heard. You've reached the final stretch, my friend, and it won't be long before you're a dad. Just enough time to tie up those last few stray ends; and get a move on with finishing the bathroom – you really are pushing it for time now.

7. Counting Down The Days

she's as big
as a cow

So you've attended the antenatal classes, winced at the stirrups, and maybe even done a few dummy runs to the hospital. You're aware that you should be prepared for things to start moving anytime from a few weeks before your baby's due date. Now it's really building up to the big climax and you're starting to get really twitchy. There are just those few final things to sort out first.

The Birth Plan

This is a kind of questionnaire for your partner to fill in regarding the kind of delivery she would like, usually supplied by the hospital or her NCT class or her local practice. When she first arrives home with her blank birthing plan, you might well be impressed with the level of personalization that prospective parents can request for the delivery. From decisions about having the baby in the squat position to intravenous drugs, it's all there for the choosing. It's well worth thinking about the answers before you write them down; but let's just hope they actually pay a blind bit of notice to what you put down!

Your partner's birth plan (and it is hers, not yours) is her statement of intent to the midwives and doctors that are going to be present at the birth. It is good to have this in written form as she is not going to be capable of giving a reasoned answer regarding positions and pain relief whilst in the throes of labour. She will list what sort of labour she wants, things that she would like to occur and things that she most definitely does not want to occur. It is, of course, quite difficult to write a birth plan, as your partner does not know what is actually going to happen; especially with regard to how she will react to the pain, how long the labour is going to last, and if there are going to be any complications.

Assuming there are no emergencies, the midwife will try to stick to the spirit of the plan, if not the letter. You might be hard-pushed to get them to include the bit about the bikini-clad women tossing rose petals over the new-born baby whilst chanting your name, or is that just me? When push comes to shove, so to speak, the midwife will always act in the best interest of your baby. If your partner's plans are overridden, then there is generally a very good reason for this and it is unlikely to be the spiteful result of that rather loutish comment you made early on in the labour, or that the midwife doesn't like the look of you, despite your insistence on wearing the Groucho Marx moustache and novelty glasses.

Keep Things Realistic

Certainly help your partner to write the birth plan, and more importantly try to understand why she is making the decisions she is, but bear in mind that it might all end up completely different. How many New Year's resolutions have you made over the years that haven't quite gone to plan?

Choosing a birthing position, for instance, is a pretty monumental decision. It could take weeks for her to decide upon, and then she may well change her mind at the last minute. You are going to be there to witness all of this, so it is important you are aware of the decisions being made even if they are not your particular first choice in the matter.

It is possible that the birth plan may be the cause of an argument or two in your household. Pregnant women tend to write their birth plan in a very 'earth mother' way. The emphasis tends to be on what is best for the baby (this is not a bad thing) and their own welfare is often put on hold. This is especially the case regarding pain relief. Your input will be much closer to what the doctors would prefer was written. You are looking to make the best of a bad situation, for both your baby and your partner. That's why blokes tend to be all for pain relief, and lots of it, because they are not looking forward to seeing their partner suffer. The birth plan will involve some compromise on both your parts (with you probably compromising more than her), but your major role is to be the logic in the partnership when the actual time comes; the doctors, midwives and your partner may well need you to make important decisions at the birth.

Water Babies

One of the different birth options increasingly available is the water birth. If your partner is considering this she may, quite literally, pretend to give birth in the bath. And you may well be horrified by the idea. I had a recurring nightmare of a blood-filled Olympic swimming pool, complete with ten competing athletes, all fighting for personal bests in the 200m breaststroke, while in the corner Lisa, me, and a couple of midwives were getting tangled in the baby's huge, snake-like, umbilical cord. Would the baby drown between birth and being raised, like a fleshy Titanic, from the water? What if the baby took too long to come out and was flooded with water while still in the vagina? What if the water was too cold? Of course none of these things ever happen; if they did it is highly unlikely, in these litigious times, that so many hospitals would now be offering the service. In fact, all the evidence shows that, if you can manage it, water births are one of the least painful and most pleasant ways to deliver a child.

Water births are heralded as a real step in the right direction with regard to natural pain relief. Your partner will be able to move around more easily in water and the ambient temperature has a very soothing effect on contractions. Despite my personal fears, there is of course no danger of injury to baby or mother during the process, any more than there is when having a baby on terra firma. It probably helps if the midwife has her 25-metre swimming badge though. The few fathers that I interviewed who had witnessed a water birth, felt that being in the water with their partner allowed them to feel more involved with the labour and birth, but few have been comfortable with the idea of having a bath ever since. One father reported that refraction meant that his new-born baby resembled Godzilla as he was brought out of his partner's vagina and up to the surface.

He was a tad frightened.

Water births can be granted for first pregnancies. A lot will depend on whether the midwife has the right kind of experience and whether she suspects any complications such as breech birth. Facilities at your local hospitals will also determine, quite early on, whether this is even a viable option. Most midwives will actively encourage water births as they are strong believers in a chance for a dip, and of course the relaxing benefits of water for both mum and baby alike. Water births may be discouraged if your partner has previously had a caesarean section; all matters like this can be discussed with the midwife.

You can even opt for a water birth at home, but this will require your midwife agreeing. The equipment can be hired relatively cheaply, but I imagine it depends on the size of your house whether this is in any way a practical and realistic option.

'Yes, over there by the TV please!'

The Best-Laid Plans ...

Lisa decided to opt for a water birth; I held my tongue, and decided she knew best. When Alia became overdue by a matter of two weeks, a date for induction was set – and our option for a water birth, indeed the entire contents of our birth plan, were ignored. This was mainly because Lisa's labour was so brief; there simply wasn't the time, or the staff on hand, to grant the request. We went from lush water birth, surrounded by the scent of jasmine and juniper, flickering candles and a soundtrack of dolphins and whales, to Delivery Suite 4, a metal bed, and lots of plastic sheets. The only water in the room was breaking all over the tiled floor.

Gary, one father interviewed, reported that his wife Jane had opted for a water birth and everything was arranged accordingly, until Jane went into labour and reported to the hospital. Through some strange mix-up, the birthing pool was delivered to the wrong ward, and the labour progressed so quickly that, Jane gave birth naturally in a maternity suite. As mentioned, nothing is set in stone. Talk to any number of parents and you will hear many similar stories. The birth plan is just that – a plan.

Home Birth

Home births are becoming more and more popular. We tend to forget that until relatively recently babies were always born at home. But for many blokes this brings worry, because these were also times when the risk of losing mother and/or baby during childbirth were quite high. Thankfully this is no longer the case.

Most midwives will be as comfortable delivering a baby in your home as they are in a hospital. It will be decided early on in your partner's pregnancy whether a home birth is an option open to you. Martin witnessed his first baby being born at home. The labour was particularly long and he and his partner were both grateful that they had everything they needed, in terms of snacks and drinks, in the kitchen. When the contractions were constant, but not too painful, the two of them were able to sit and watch a movie – Martin was grateful that he didn't have to spend this time in a hospital. As the hours went on, his partner moved up to the bedroom with the midwife; Martin had to stop himself from nipping downstairs to get a beer, or worse, turning on the television for the football scores. As the baby's birth approached there were some minor complications that led to a lot of blood loss, but the midwife dealt efficiently with these and a healthy baby boy was born. Martin's advice is not to choose the room with the fancy pine furniture and cream carpets – the room looked more like an abattoir than a bedroom when all was said and done.

Home births will certainly help your partner feel more relaxed during the labour and delivery if they are not particularly fond of hospitals. If she is keen and the midwife gives the go-ahead, there is no reason to worry. Just keep off the PlayStation during important moments! And if there are any complications with the birth, the midwife will have your partner transported to hospital immediately to ensure the best medical attention is provided. In fact medical back-up will be on hand for all home births, just in case. If this does happen it can be very frustrating and disappointing for the two of you, as was the case for John and Paula, who needed such back-up after Paula had endured 22 hours of labour at home. So close, and yet so far.

Caesarean Section

At the other end of the 'natural birth' spectrum is the caesarean section. It's becoming all the rage nowadays, or at least that's what the experts are saying. In the UK we are looking at about 15 per cent of babies being born by caesarean section. In the US it accounts for almost 30 per cent of all babies born. What is quite a major operation is becoming a more on-demand commodity by the year. The whole question of caesareans has become politicized in the past few years, as natural-birth advocates argue that many are unnecessarily taking place simply because it is cheaper and more convenient for the doctors (and the mothers) to know in advance exactly when and how the baby will be born – it certainly cuts out a lot of hanging around. The fact that many women would understandably prefer to avoid the pain and discomfort of labour should also not be discounted. But most caesareans will take place for purely medical reasons.

In some cases, your partner will know in advance of labour that the baby is going to be born by caesarean section. This is usually the case if the baby is in the breech position, if there are more than three babies, if the placenta is blocking the baby's exit, or if the mother has a history of caesarean sections. It may also be so if your partner is of a particularly small stature and the baby is likely to be very large, (a King-Edward-potato size baby would be large, as far as I am concerned).

In emergency cases, caesarean sections are carried out if your baby's heartbeat suddenly becomes irregular, which would suggest that he or she is in some distress and may not survive a vaginal delivery. If, during labour or even delivery, it becomes apparent that the umbilical cord is wrapped around the baby's neck, posing a very real choking risk, then a caesarean section will be carried out. Other rea- sons include the placenta tearing, the baby being unable to move any further because the cervix has stopped dilating, or the umbilical cord prolapsing, which increases the chance of it becoming compressed during delivery and therefore possibly cutting off your baby's blood supply.

In The Theatre

Fathers' reactions to caesarean sections vary for a number of reasons. Some hated it but most actually enjoyed it. Those who enjoyed it appreciated the fact that they were allowed to be present in the operating theatre, and that they were screened from the gory details but were still able to provide support at their partner's side. From a purely selfish point of view, the fathers often get to hold the baby first once it is delivered, whilst the surgeon completes the stitching up. Some even enjoyed the chance to dress up in ill-fitting scrubs. (I'm not sure why, but each to his own!)

It must be said that whether it is a scheduled caesarean or an emergency procedure it will probably be extremely quick. A huge comfort is the number of staff on hand to help and this is reassuring, particularly for dad – luckily, any paranoia you might have otherwise experienced is not given the chance to develop. The operation, in the majority of cases, takes less than half an hour. Nobody likes to see their partner in agony, and on the occasions where there are complications with the labour and an emergency caesarean is decided upon after many hours of labour, it can actually be a relief. You may have a horrible fear during a long (and sometimes during a short) labour that your partner might not survive the experience and that you will be left alone with a new-born baby. Having become very used to the same four walls for the last 17 hours, it can be a shock to the system to suddenly have to put on scrubs and literally run after your partner being wheeled across the maternity suite.

'Don't forget to bring a nappy and some clothes for your baby,' comes the cry from the midwife. Then the fact that your baby is imminent finally becomes real. After such a long and arduous wait, your child is finally coming. Flustered, you might find it difficult to open the zip on the hold-all to retrieve the nappy and clothes.

If you are worried about the possibility of an emergency caesarean, take heart from the story of a French couple, Thierry and Helen. They recounted that at first Helen was giving birth naturally and everything was fine. But Helen is particularly small and the midwife soon realized that the baby could simply travel no further. Helen was taken for an emergency caesarean and the baby was pulled back up into the womb and then out. Thierry had been worried that, at some stage, he might be asked to choose between

Helen and the baby, but the caesarean solved the problem. Unpleasant, yes, but unpleasantness that saved the day.

The downside of a caesarean is that it is a major operation and will cause major trauma to your partner's body. She will be incapacitated for days, at the one time she could really do with being fighting fit (many women say they are not completely back to normal for a few months). Finally, if the caesarean is unplanned some women feel sad about 'missing out'; they feel cheated of a natural birth. For a few mums, feeling that they will be branded 'too posh to push', like all those celebrity mothers, is a pain worse than the operation itself. In this situation it's best to simply focus on the end result: look at your beautiful baby and realize that they are all that matters. How they made it here is, ultimately, irrelevant.

Breech Birth

I was a breech birth and I lived to tell this tale, so it can't be all that bad. (Mum, of course, might argue differently.) My father has always maintained that I came out arse first, and that I've subsequently done everything in my life in the same manner … I am sure he doesn't mean it.

My mother remembers a midwife who was not involved with my birth commenting on me in the maternity ward: 'You can always tell a breech birth, they're the prettiest babies.' To which my father now retorts: 'Yes, but look what happened.' Charmed, I'm sure.

As the pregnancy nears completion, around about eight months, your baby will settle on the position that makes the best use of the space available. For the vast majority of babies this is the vertex position, which means vertical with the head facing down, or quite simply upside down. Fussier babies (about three in every hundred), myself included, who assert their independence even *in utero*, decide that they would much rather be head up and bottom down – precisely how we are supposed to be in the outside world, so why not get the practise in now.

This might be how your baby decides he is more comfortable, but it is not ideal for your partner. If things progress without any intervention, then it is going to be baby's bum or feet that come out first, followed by the coconut of a head. Ouch.

Most doctors or midwives will manually attempt to alter the baby's position to the more favoured vertex position (externally … for once!), which works almost half the time for first-time mothers, and more often if your partner has had a baby before. In these cases, and as long as baby doesn't roll back, cheekily, when no one is looking, then everything continues as normal and your child will be delivered head first.

If manual rotation is not successful, then most hospitals will advise that the baby should be born by caesarean section. They do, of course, have the baby's best interests at heart, but they are also incredibly scared of litigation. Breech births carry a greater risk of fatalities and injuries and that is why your doctor may advise against a vaginal birth. Some midwives would counter-argue that breech births are completely acceptable and that by forcing caesarean sections we are inadvertently deskilling trainees – the argument continues. Most importantly, it is still possible for your partner to deliver vaginally, but she may have to find a midwife who is experienced and willing to work with her.

Trawling the Internet, I found that mothers who had experienced breech-birth babies swore (probably very loudly) that water births were fantastic for this very type of delivery. The water of the pool was similar to the amniotic fluid, and as mother and baby were so relaxed, he or she just slipped out. Further delving might have revealed that the breech- birth baby was in fact baby number twelve and that number eleven had been born in the car, on the way to Bingo, with- out causing mum to miss a gear shift.

How you deal with this eventuality is a decision that can't be taken lightly. But remember, that pretty face will be the envy of the maternity ward!

Be Prepared!

Towards the end of the third trimester you won't be alone if you are a little bit bored of the whole affair. Frankly, your partner is probably bored stiff with it too. The last few weeks can really seem to drag and us blokes just want the whole birth bit over and done with. It really is worse than waiting for Christmas or a birthday when you are a child – afterwards, of course, you will both look back and think that the nine months flew by; indeed after your twentieth night on the trot with no sleep you might even wish that you could wind back the clock. But those final weeks drag. You're not able to venture too far from home, but yet another day passes without incident.

There is little you can do to speed up the process but you can ensure that you are prepared. By now your partner will have filled a rucksack suitable for scaling the north face of Everest. You will know this because it will probably be left at the bottom of the stairs for you to trip over. It is filled with various items that it has been recommended she brings along for the birth. Trust me, that contents list will not include items suitable for you. To pass the time, and as a practical accessory that you may or may not require, I would advise you to fill up a small bag with the following:

- Change (and lots of it) for the hospital car park
- Red Bull or similar caffeine-based drink (the coffee at

hospitals, assuming the dispenser is working, is horrible)
- Chocolate and crisps – your favourite flavours
- Spare T-shirt
- Deodorant
- Toothbrush and toothpaste
- Sandwich
- Phone
- Tissue for the tears (you think I'm joking)

You'll be pleased you've done it when the time comes, and let's be honest, it killed a good twenty minutes looking around the house for all those coins.

Responsibility Kicks In

Most strikingly the final weeks before the pregnancy are a time of realization. Your home is looking the cleanest that it has ever been. All those annoying DIY jobs are now done, (well most of them, anyway), and you are both really looking forward to seeing some of the equipment that has been bought in for the baby actually being put to use.

It all seems to be fitting together nicely, and in the grand scheme of things you still haven't had to lift a finger. Your worries about money, marriage, sex, and life in general have subsided considerably. Responsibility, it seems, is not so bad after all. You will now be quite used to your partner's various demands, and, on occasion may even be able to predict a few of them.

Take the time to look around the house and listen to the silence. It is absolutely bizarre that in a matter of weeks, or maybe even days, this home that you have made is about to welcome a new arrival. One father mentioned that his most profound moment before the birth was washing the baby's clothes (as is recommended). Touching these clothes was an extraordinary experience; they were at the same time both small (compared to adult clothing) and huge, and very soon would be filled.

And before you have time to catch your breath, you realize that the time has come...

8. Birth – The Big One

Imagine this: it's 11.30 p.m., you've had a few glasses of wine and you've spoken to friends all night on the phone. Your partner has gone to bed for another early night. You are really looking forward to the birth, but there's a week to go. Everything is relaxed. Until your partner comes into the room looking sleepy but excited.

'We have to go to the hospital now.'

Imagine this: you're busy at work, it's a couple of hours after lunch and therefore a couple of hours before you can go home. Your boss is particularly chatty today and you're relieved that you have someone to help you prepare the big presentation to the board next week. Suddenly your boss glances down at your desk and picks off a sticky note from your monitor. It says, 'Call Wife Now.' Fighting through traffic you race to get home.

Imagine this: your wife complains she is in pain and the two of you drive to the hospital. You book in and someone is busy attaching various wires to her tummy. Eight hours later you are a dad.

How you will learn that the baby is coming will probably be as unique as the child itself. Hopefully, you will be nearby, prepared and will both know what to look out for.

Waiting For The Phone Call

Now that we want, and are expected, to be part of the birth process, the image of the man pacing outside a delivery suite has been replaced by the image of him pacing around work, unable to concentrate on anything, waiting for the phone to ring. It could happen at any time (and you really hope that it does happen before the presentation you have to make to the board this afternoon). The due date was a week ago, but still the suspense is there. We're an impatient bunch and you won't be the first to ask your partner, 'So when's this baby actually coming?'

By this stage she will be even more desperate to have baby on the outside than you; shouting at her won't really help the situation much, but it might make you feel better.

'The Show'

Your partner will usually be alerted to the onset of labour in one of three ways. 'The show' is essentially a plug, made up of mucus, which has been protecting your baby's watery world for the past months by forming a barrier in the cervical canal. As the cervix begins its radical change in size in preparation for the baby to be born, the plug becomes redundant and is dislodged and expelled. This is a painless experience (although the contraction that dislodged it most probably was not), and is one reason to start making your preparations for the hospital. It is not uncommon for 'the show' to be accompanied by a small amount of blood.

Although it is almost as imprecise as the 'how long is a piece of string' maxim, medical sources say that if any blood present constitutes no more than a stain then there is absolutely nothing to worry about. If, however, there is a 'considerable amount' of blood, it is imperative that you contact your midwife or the hospital immediately. Also remember that 'the show' could be expelled weeksbefore the actual birth, so it is not a sure sign of labour, merely a possible sign.

Breaking Of The Waters

Officially known as 'rupture of the membranes', thanks to countless films and books the breaking of the waters is often mistakenly regarded as the 'official' sign that labour has begun. However, labour might not properly begin until quite a few hours after your partner's waters have broken. In fact it may not even begin at all, without being induced. However, it is a sign that things are progressing and that labour may well be about to start. The fathers interviewed described the waters variously as either a spectacular torrent or a slow trickle. Some women are convinced that they have heard theirs actually 'pop'. Either way, it is now time to contact, if not go to, the hospital; your baby's birth is imminent. If you have opted for a home birth then your midwife will need to be alerted.

Be careful if the waters break where you have lino or laminated flooring; you can't afford for either of you to have a nasty fall at this crucial stage! Another tip for the mother is never to lock the bathroom door. Kate suddenly found herself completely incapacitated by the onset of labour, and to cap it all the lock on her bathroom door, always dodgy at the best of times, had completely jammed, leaving her trapped. Having six burly firemen knocking down your bathroom door may be near the top of most women's fantasies, but the effect is entirely spoilt when you are nine months pregnant and wallowing around the floor like a beached whale.

Contractions

Much as an atlas of the world, or a globe, has longitudinal and latitudinal lines, so your partner's uterus is lined with a veritable gridiron of muscles. During the labour they will contract, helping to position your baby ready for birth. But again, how long is a piece of string? There are contractions and there are *contractions*. At which stage do you judge that it is time to go to the hospital, or contact the midwife? Early contractions tend to be felt, but they do not cause actual pain. This is not labour, just your partner's body getting ready. If, however, your partner finds the contractions painful and they feel different to those that might have occurred in the last weeks of pregnancy, causing her to concentrate on her breathing, then it is time to go to the hospital. If you are keeping count, then it is recommended that once the contractions are lasting about a minute and occurring every five to ten minutes, then it is time to go into hospital.

The Hospital Dash

Along with her waters breaking in the middle of the super- market, the dramatic emergency dash to the hospital through frenetic traffic is one of the more enduring images of labour. Fathers who were denied this experience – such as those whose partners were induced, or had planned caesareans – even talked of 'feeling cheated' in some way. If you do get to live out the cliché, no matter how much you have gone over the route in your mind, or even in practice, actually driving in a car with a woman who is about to give birth will create an awful lot of pressure. Expect your driving to be erratic at best, and some of the choice language that might escape your lips to be forever memorable.

If this were a medical text then I would have to mention something about not drinking alcohol at all, or at least in moderation. But it's not, and most of us like a drink to one extent or another. This, thankfully, is not really an issue during the pregnancy for us blokes until about four weeks before the due date, when, let's face it, you could become a dad at any moment. It may be easy for you or it may be hard, but from about week 36 until the baby is born, if you are the designated driver for the hospital run, you simply cannot get drunk, let alone still be over the limit when you are called to duty in the early hours of the morning. There really would be nothing worse than missing the birth of your child by spending a night in the local cells, coupled with not being able to drive a car for at least a year – never mind the horrific thought of possibly injuring your partner, your baby, or someone else!

Nick, one of my interviewees, likes to think he's a bit of a lad. Bit of a prat is how his partner Sonia would probably put it. Nick was determined that the small matter of his baby being due any day was not going to cramp his drinking style. The night of his mate's birthday was a particularly big one, and of course would be the very night that Sonia began to feel the unmistakable pangs. She then had to try and wake her comatose partner up, carry him to the car, and drive him to the hospital in the middle of the night. Not the easiest thing to do when you're doubling over in pain. Unsurprisingly, they've since split up.

Personally, I think that it would be a good idea to issue women who are seven months pregnant a special siren or bright pink light powered by the cigarette lighter in the car. It would be understood that anyone using said light would be on their way to hospital to give birth, giving every expectant father, for one day only (or maybe a few days if the labour is false) complete dominance on the road with powers that hitherto were only enjoyed by the emergency services. Like everything else, this idea would be abused, but it would be nice to at least pilot the scheme.

'False' Labour

The gap of time between your partner feeling those first strong contractions and being 'fully dilated' can lead to a so-called 'false labour' which can be pretty embarrassing for both you and your partner. You feel as if you are wasting everyone's time, or jumping the gun, even though you may well have been asked to come in by your midwife. After your mad dash to the hospital, you had imagined that the next time you left the hospital it would be as a family of three, and your partner would look a lot smaller ... but no, it's home once more and, for most men, the painful long march back to work. To add insult to injury, nobody's happy to see you back so soon, especially not without some new- born baby photos!

For Steve, the situation became very like the boy that cried wolf. Having been to the hospital four times in as many days, on the fifth day when his wife called he decided not to rush the large lunch that he had just ordered. By the time he collected his wife from home, they had all of 23 minutes between arriving at the hospital and his son being born. Close.

Although you will both feel a bit daft, false labours are not a waste of time or resources. You might feel that you would like your partner to stay in the hospital, once you get there even though nothing is happening, but you really are better off going home and waiting there. If it is your first child, you are likely to be looking at the same four walls for far longer than is good for you anyway; don't add to that time. At home, you have all the comforts you and your partner need and the familiar surroundings will help her relax far more than the bland hospital ward would.

If you have been sent home once, the next time you go back you kind of expect it to happen again – and it is almost a shock when the midwife informs you that they are keeping your partner in for the night.

'Is it coming then?' you ask.

'Your baby will be born tomorrow!' Help!

The countdown has begun.

Induction – Or, You're Coming Out Whether You Like It Or Not

Sometimes things don't happen like that at all. Sometimes your baby is quite happy to stay in the womb longer than is entirely necessary and healthy. It makes sense really; it's warm, cosy and has been home for all the baby's life – why rock the boat? Well, unfortunately to stay any longer than the usual 39 to 41 weeks can be detrimental to both mother and child. It's all those wacky dates again. Whether your partner's doctor used 'Naegele's Rule' or an ultrasound scan to determine the due date of your baby can have an impact on the accuracy of that date. 'Naegele's Rule' assumes that your partner's menstrual cycle is regular, and adds nine months and seven days to the first day of your partner's last period. An ultrasound scan will use essential measurements of your baby and the date is worked out accordingly. Neither are 100 per cent accurate all of the time and that is why babies are born early or late, for no reason other than the due date was inaccurate.

As both methods of prediction are not an exact science, inductions are commonplace, with somewhere in the region of one in five babies being born in the UK after an induced labour. Mistakes do happen and many a baby has not come out on time, because 'on time' is actually a few weeks early. Induction is a procedure that is used to bring on labour, most commonly when the baby goes two weeks past her due date. Your partner's doctor may also advise induction if the risks of prolonging the pregnancy are more serious than the risks of delivering the baby right away, if your baby has stopped growing in the uterus, if the placenta appears to be no longer functioning, or if your partner has an illness that threatens the health of the baby. For whatever reason it is time for your baby to be born, and the doctors are simply helping that process along.

There are various methods employed to induce labour, the most common being listed below. You could always try the more natural and less-invasive methods first; they might be fun if nothing else.

Curry And Spice

It might well be an old wives' tale, but who cares if it means one more chance to go for a nice meal for two before the imminent arrival. I am unclear as to why a good hot curry might aid labour; but having said that, my pushing technique the next morning can only be described as 'like giving birth'. If the effect is in any way similar for pregnant women, I can see their point.

Getting Jiggy With It – Again!

Isn't nature great! It was sex that started this whole thing off, and now you can try to finish it in exactly the same way. Sex can help in two ways when it comes to bringing on labour. The sexual act can trigger the release of the hormone oxytocin, which is the 'contraction' hormone. Although you might feel that you are giving her the best night of her life, she might actually be going into labour! Your semen also contains prostaglandins which, like a pessary, will help to soften the cervix, making it ready to dilate once contractions start. Given the choice of a pessary or sex, I know which I'd prefer.

Walking

Probably not exactly what she feels like at this precise moment, but a long walk (not too long, in case you both need to nip back to the car to go to the hospital!) will occasionally help labour start. Walking can help in two ways; if your baby has engaged then the baby's head will push down on the cervix during the walk, which might start the process off. If your baby is still to engage then walking and gravity may help to get him/her into the correct position.

Whilst not as much fun as sex, you might want to make this a joint pursuit if you can.

Ripple The Nipple!

Another top remedy from nature herself. Your partner may think you've made this one up; you haven't; just blame me. Nipple stimulation is a bit of a long shot, but it might help her body to release oxytocin, much like the drug syntocin, but without any need of drip feed, and the corresponding pain associated with the latter. Although you risk a cheeky squirt from one or both nipples, as they will be primed for use, it is worth the effort, especially if you can combine it with sex; or perhaps walking, if you are both that way inclined.

Alas, if your partner's doctor or midwife feels that your nights of spicy food and spicy sex aren't quite having the desired effect, then they will usually elect to employ less enjoyable methods of inducing labour, including:

Sweep Of The Membranes

A stretch or sweep of the membranes (the amniotic sac) that surrounds your baby is a procedure initiated by either a doctor or a midwife during an internal examination. Much like the Imperial Fleet hunting the Millennium Falcon in the asteroid field, the midwife 'tests the water', so to speak, by sweeping a finger (gloved!) across the cervix. The aim is for this to help release hormones called prostaglandins, which may 'kick-start' the labour. If the membrane sweep is successful, labour should start within the following 24 to 48 hours. It has a higher chance of working if the cervix is already softening and preparing for labour. In uncomplicated pregnancies, it will not cause any harm to either your partner or your baby. The procedure itself is not very pleasant – but not half as unpleasant as the birth itself!

A sweep is often the first option of induction employed because it is the simplest. It has proven to be very effective, and as it does not involve any medication or apparatus it is by far the preferred option.

ARM Or Breaking The Waters

Artificially rupturing the membranes (sometimes called ARM or 'breaking the waters') is another procedure that is administered during an internal examination. The doctor passes a long thin probe (much like a knitting needle, with a funny-looking hook) through the cervix just far enough to put a small break in the amniotic sac or membranes.

In a sense, the breaking of the waters is a point of no return. Whilst it might not be successful in itself in inducing the labour, you can rest assured that birth will happen within 24 hours, because after that time, there would be serious risk to the health of the baby with a ruptured membrane, it is essential that your partner gives birth soon, by natural means or other. Most dads whose babies have reached and breached their due date by as much as two weeks, will feel a wonderful feeling of relief and closure on knowing that birth is imminent, no matter how unpleasant the actual induction might be for you to observe. (And remember how much worse it is for your partner to experience.)

Pessary And Syntocin

Another very common and effective method of induction is the insertion of a pessary, or gel, containing prostaglandin into the vagina and onto the cervix. Alia, our daughter, was born after an induced labour and it really is an unpleasant experience watching a nurse shove her hand into your partner, no matter how much K-Y Jelly is about. I really didn't know where to put my eyes.

More often than not your partner will go into labour after a pessary induction. The hormone causes the contractions to start and it should all be plain sailing from then on. If things still aren't happening she will probably be given syntocin. This is a synthetic form of the hormone oxytocin. Administered through an intravenous drip, the hormone will cause contractions to begin. Because the drug is administered intravenously, once contractions have begun the rate of the drip can be altered so that contractions can, to a certain extent, be controlled.

Emergency Deliveries

At one extreme – and this is pregnancy, there are always extremes – you have the baby who does not want to come out, and at the other you have the one who simply can't wait – not for the doctors, not for the midwives and maybe not even for a comfortable place for mother to lie down. I don't mean to scare all those fathers-to-be out there who can't even stomach an episode of *ER*, but it is best to read up about emergency deliveries just in case. It is extremely unlikely that you will ever be put in the situation of having to deliver the baby yourself, but you don't want to tempt fate by not even bothering to gen up about it, do you …?

However it happens, however you got to this stage, eventually you will hear the words, 'Quick it's coming.' And that leads us quite nicely to the best bit of the whole affair
– the birth.

The First Stage Of Labour

The first stage of labour involves the onset of regular contractions and the dilation of the cervix; ideally the latter needs to dilate to ten centimetres in preparation for the baby's head. There are no hard-and-fast rules as to how long the first stage of

labour will last, but most women will agree that any length of time is too long. Be prepared for it to be as short as thirty minutes or as long as twenty-plus hours! If this is your partner's first child, labour is likely to take longer than if she has given birth before; but there are of course always exceptions to the rules. For many women the first stage of labour will begin at home and your doctor will recommend that you stay there for as long as possible. When you do finally arrive at the maternity ward, whether it be a scheduled induction or a rushed, still-in- your-pyjamas mad dash, you might be forgiven for thinking
that everyone is taking it all a bit too casually.

Can I Have Your Attention Please?

Although it is difficult to be objective in this situation, the nursing staff, midwives and doctors on duty are highly trained professionals and (despite probably a very long shift) know almost instinctively when it is time to rush around panicking and when it is best to let nature take its course. Your partner will be examined very quickly to determine whether labour has begun, although you might both feel you are waiting around unduly.

It is important to realize that there will be other women in the ward whose needs are greater at that precise moment; it could be another hour or even another 24 hours before your baby is born. If labour has begun, staff will hook up machinery to monitor your baby's heartbeat. You might feel that your partner is being ignored, but that really is not the case. You are well within your rights to ask for some more assistance, but there is probably nothing else that anyone can do. Both you and your partner will have to wait for the contractions to start getting stronger and more frequent. When they do, you'll know about it.

Monitoring The Heartbeat

A quick note on baby monitors, a common cause of fear in dads. They slip off, at least once or twice, and if your partner is thrashing around, possibly even more. I was not the only father to be horrified when I saw the flat line on my baby's heart-rate. With a non-committal glance, the midwife looked at the monitor, looked at Lisa's belly, and then carried on writing her notes, her first novel, or whatever it was that seemed much more interesting than what appeared to be a cardiac arrest. Did I mention a word? No, not even a whimper. I was struck dumb, as much by the midwife's reaction as with the event I thought that I was witnessing. Thankfully, the monitor was replaced and the heartbeat was again audible and visible. Baby monitors can become a huge annoyance to your partner. There are a lot of wires and equipment involved with childbirth and some, if not all, will be connected to one part or another of your partner's body. The connections are itchy and uncomfortable and the stress of hearing that little blip – or not hearing it – for hours on end can really add to the tension. Of course they are also doing a vital job, and if there are any complications with the birth you'll thank your lucky stars for all this modern technology.

Birds, Hands And Bushes

Just about the time you are ready to get extremely angry and complain that, after many hours, no one seems particularly interested in looking after your partner, help arrives. It is when help arrives that you decide you would have preferred it if they had stayed outside. A lot of men react with utter disbelief as a number of midwives and possibly even a doctor or two (or several, if there are pre-med students in town) begin to examine your partner vaginally. Often abrupt, and just a tad disconcerting (for your partner as well, I am sure!) the very basic procedure of sticking (gloved) fingers into your partner's vagina will establish approximately how far labour has progressed.

It is likely that this examination will have to be repeated a number of times during the labour, until the cervix has dilated to the required ten-centimetre diameter. It is, quite honestly, hard to know exactly where to look; most of you will probably be focusing on the doctor, making sure that there is not even a hint of enjoyment written on his face.

Would You Not Prefer To Lie Down?

In certain circumstances your partner will be required to stay on the bed, but to ease her pain she may prefer to walk around the delivery room, or rest in what can only be described as bizarre positions against walls, beds or chairs. If you are called into the hospital from work or somewhere else, do not be surprised if the sight that greets you is your beloved on all fours, crawling around the floor in her pants. It is probably better not to show shock or disapproval at this and instead to try to comfort her as best you can.

Standing upright, on her head, squatting, or any other position that your partner decides is right at that moment, is right. A combination of contractions, the baby moving, and anxiety will all mean that your partner wants to remain as comfortable as possible, and this will not usually be horizontal on a bed. You may be required to provide support for her arms and shoulders if a squat is assumed. Likewise, if you don't get your hand bitten off, you may wish to rub areas of your partner's lower back to ease some of the pressure. There are no wrongs and rights, but some simple dialogue and possibly advice from the midwife will point you in the right direction – or at least leave a lasting impression in your mind that touching her back, right then, was a really bad thing to do!

The Key To The Cabinet Please, Matron

As described in the previous chapter, there will be a whole cacophony of pain relief available for your partner to help her through labour. No doubt she will have decided what she requires when she prepares her birth plan. This is when the existence of two very distinct camps becomes evident: the 'natural' camp and the 'needle in the spine? I love it!' camp.

As I might have mentioned, if it was me having a baby I'd probably make sure that I received every drug available, convince the midwife or nurse to double the quantities and possibly even try to acquire a little something extra from that bloke that stands by the fruit machine in the local. I am a self-confessed wimp and have fond memories of morphine's incredible effects on me as a teenager (in a hospital setting I hasten to add, officer). Natural or needle? I would be the one with the tourniquet round my arm, slapping my inner elbow to get the veins up long before the first contraction had even begun. Most blokes agree that they would opt for an epidural immediately, and with a few hours to go until the birth would most probably want their Gameboy with them too. That said, maybe if they were actually giving birth themselves they might not be so gung-ho. While we might like the idea of being born stoned, would we really wish it on our new baby?

But there are those (ladies, you're mad) who want to feel

everything and have their baby with the least amount of intervention possible. Perhaps they're not that keen on needles (especially one as long as your arm being shoved into your spinal column). Whichever camp your partner falls into, it is probably going to be your job to insist on, or refuse, pain relief on behalf of your partner when the time comes. To keep you on your toes, if she is on the 'natural' ticket before contractions, she might well alter her stance after, say, 17 hours of labour. Discuss this one and make sure you really do know what it is she wants, or doesn't want.

Speak Now, Or Forever Hold Your Peace

When it comes to the greatest goal ever scored, or why the boss is such an incompetent buffoon, we're assertive blokes who say what's on our mind. That is, until we're stood like a lemon next to our partner who is about to give birth to our baby. Coupled with the feeling of inadequacy will be the fear that we really don't know what on earth we can do to help, especially as the knowledge about birth contained in the midwife's little finger is more than we could ever hope to learn in a lifetime.

It's probably easier to blow a bugle, wearing a fur coat, in front of 250 hunt saboteurs than it is to speak up in the delivery room, but that's what you will have to do if things are not progressing the way you or your partner wants them to. You have to be the voice of two, because right at this moment she is doubtless in a fair amount of pain, and suggesting that you might be illegitimate, which isn't really progressing the situation much. If you don't know, ask, and if you want to know more, ask.

And Remember To Breathe!

This is where all those antenatal classes come into play. If

you attended the class or at least read the books, you will be aware
of the importance of breathing correctly during contractions. It is,
of course, incredibly important that you breathe correctly through
your partner's labour and the birth, or you might pass out, but the
lessons and guide- books are to ensure that your partner breathes
correctly.

All that huffing and puffing felt ridiculous in front of the
other expectant couples and probably even worse if you tried it
alone in the house. But if your partner holds her breath she will
not be allowing each contraction to do its job properly, and will
not be getting enough oxygen to bring energy into her own, and
the baby's body. Likewise, breathing too fast will cause an
imbalance of oxygen and carbon dioxide, possibly resulting in
hyperventilation, leading in turn to dizziness and pins and needles.
The breathing techniques are there to force a rhythm and to avoid
the breaths becoming too shallow or too deep. You should take a
leading role, and if you notice your partner is not breathing
rhythmically, insist that she pays attention to you and follows your
lead. Getting your partner to pay attention to you may also help
take the edge off some of the pain she is feeling. Now is not the
time to be feeling shy in front of the midwives. They have seen it all
before and encourage maximum involvement on your part.

The Second Stage Of Labour

It is fabled that during labour, husbands and partners get called
every name under the sun. It's true! And what is worse is that it is
not just every name under our sun, but includes derogatory terms
not even invented yet in this galaxy. You are the root cause for all
this pain, suffering and inconvenience. And pay for it you will.

'Without you this wouldn't be happening. Right now,

I really feel the need to shout at someone – and as you aren't doing anything useful, you are going to be the target of my abuse for the next couple of minutes.' If you thought that your partner was quite quiet and choosy with her vocabulary then it is likely that you will be introduced, quite suddenly and personally, to the dark side of the force.

The good news is that you are now very close to becoming a father, and your partner will very soon give birth. The cervix is now fully dilated and each contraction will be helping to manoeuvre the baby into the world. Smile and nod and try not to retaliate. The midwife will usually grin at you, which doesn't help matters. Your partner really doesn't mean it. Well, actually she does, but it's only temporary. If you did walk out of the delivery suite in a huff, where would she be then? Your partner is simply getting the fear.

Getting The Fear

It was during the transition from the first to the second stage of labour that Lisa got the fear. The agony of the contractions with nothing more than gas and air to assist was taking its toll. Deep in her mind she was convinced that a first labour would last for countless hours and she had only been going for about two. The fear of much more of this was almost too much and she cried out for us to 'make it stop'. To witness your partner in any form of agony is horrid. I was very close to asking the midwife to administer some pethidine, but Lisa had categorically said that she did not want any drugs.

It is not uncommon for your partner – and you, too – to feel overwhelmed at this point. Max said his wife, a bit of a drama queen at the best of times, started begging the midwife, 'Just let me die, please. Put me out of my agony!' Rest assured that this means you have now entered the last leg of the journey and your family is about to have an additional member.

This phase is like the culmination of all the venom we first spotted in our partner in about the second trimester, coming to the fore in a big explosion. A perfect example was kindly provided by Bill and Michelle. Both were keen for a home birth, but the midwife gently refused, citing their small maisonette, which had difficult access, as a potential hazard should there be any complications. Michelle, of very slight frame, someone who cares for people and animals, kept reasonably calm. Bill soothed her annoyance (although it did take a few weeks). Kind, gentle, wouldn't- hurt-a-fly Michelle was resigned to a natural birth in hospital and even began to warm to the idea. During labour she was adamant that she did not want pain relief of any description, under any circumstances. The labour was long and arduous. At one point Bill went out of the room to get them both a glass of water. On returning he spotted Michelle, all five foot one of her, pinning the midwife up against the wall and screaming at her like a banshee: 'Give me an epidural now you f***ing bitch.' But it was too late, the labour too far advanced. Bill remained scared for a good number of weeks after the birth. The midwife, thank- fully, laughed it off. She'd seen it all, and more, before.

Can I Handle It?

Getting the fear can, of course, happen to *you* too. One interviewee admitted that during the birth of his first child he panicked, made his excuses and left the delivery room. It was simply all too much and he sought solace elsewhere. He wasn't uncaring or unkind, just completely overwhelmed by the event. Most of us will wonder if we are 'man enough' for the birth – the answer is yes. You might be sick, you might even faint, and you may well cry, but you almost certainly will remain there and it will without doubt be the most profound experience of your life.

Who Invited You?

At certain stages during the labour, there may be as many as three midwives in the room as well as a doctor. Including you and your partner, and with baby shortly to make an appearance, it will feel a little crowded and particularly hot. This can be somewhat unsettling. Is this number of people necessary, or are some of them here just to watch? You will feel both protective of your partner and worried at the same time. Thinking logically, you should be over the moon that so much knowledge and combined experience is concentrating on the well-being of your partner and baby, but of course you are not thinking rationally.

Passing Ships In The Night

It will be all action downstairs from both your partner's front and back bottom. All that pushing, all that intense concentration, will most probably mean that a surreptitious poo might make a cheeky appearance; and if you happen to catch sight of something, it's best to be forewarned. You might not even notice, as the midwife will most likely clean it up with a deft wipe or replacement of plastic sheeting. If your partner has opted for a water birth, the experience might be a little more 'in your face' and hugely reminiscent of swimming off the coast of England, or sharing a bath as a child with a sibling.

The whole birth experience is a hot and smelly affair. With all that poo, blood, mucus and flesh in the room, it's a pretty raw experience. But the end justifies the means and I think that it all adds to the beauty of birth. Let's be honest, us blokes would be the first to cack it if we were about to give birth to a nine-pound baby – and probably more than once.

Getting Hot Under The Collar

About the time that the second stage of labour is reached, someone will crank up the heat in the delivery suite to something akin to your partner's internal body temperature, in preparation for the arrival. This is simply so that when your baby is born, she will not feel as if she has been dropped into the middle of the North Atlantic. Bear in mind that your baby has been enjoying her mother's body temperature for the last nine months, and if being born weren't enough of a shock, cold air certainly would be. Your partner's ambient temperature will feel a lot like sitting on a radiator, and if you're expecting a winter baby you'll regret putting on the Christmas jumper you got from mum with the reindeer and the fur collar and cuffs. It does get uncomfortably warm, and what with all the nerves, back-rubbing, forehead-swabbing and leg-holding that you'll be doing, you'll be feeling pretty toasty yourself.

Some fathers do pass out in a delivery room and I would guess that's as much to do with overheating and exhaustion as with emotion or relief. Be warned, all the focus (quite rightly) will be on the well-being of your partner and the baby; I have heard, although this may be disputed, that if a dad does pass out they are ignored and just left on the floor to recover.

The Crowning Glory

Once your partner enters the second stage of labour, it's all hands on deck. The tempo of everyone and everything begins to take on its own peculiar rhythm. Everyone will be focused on the birth. There is a buzz of excitement in the room, and you can almost taste the anticipation (or is that breakfast saying a cheeky hello again?).

When the midwife confirms that the baby is coming, you may have already decided, quite categorically, that you are going to be standing as far away from the business end of things as humanly possible. You will focus on the face of your beloved, and ignore it all. This might not prove to be the case. The whole procedure becomes fascinating and you may well find yourself gradually getting closer and closer to all the action. When the midwife declares that the head is visible, you take it as your cue. You want to have a green cloak and facemask, and a pair of surgical gloves – you want to help. Fortunately for your partner and baby, if you do start getting in the way, the midwife will gently nudge ahead of you and deliver your baby professionally and with great speed.

And They're Out!

Once your baby crowns, and the head becomes visible, it will usually only be a matter of moments before the rest of him, or her, literally shoots across the bed, or into the water, as if fired from a cannon. No matter how long the labour, the contrast in speed when it comes to the actual birth is exhilarating and a little frightening. It might be a stroke of luck that there is an umbilical cord, to stop the poor little mite from being fired across the length of the room.

If you went to the antenatal classes you may have already seen a baby being born on film. It is an amazing sight and all the more emotional when witnessed in the flesh and the baby is yours. Even those fathers who said that they were squeamish about blood admitted that they were oblivious to the sight when the time of birth came. If at any stage you or your partner feels that nine months is a long time to wait for a baby, take my word for it that the wait is worth it. All those mornings of sickness, all those cravings, all those contractions lead to just one thing – and it's a fabulous thing indeed. And the midwives and doctors never tire of bringing new babies into the world; they will be as over the moon as you are.

That's Not Going Where I Think It's Going?

Sometimes things don't happen quite so naturally and if the baby 'gets stuck', or your partner is simply too exhaust- ed to push any more, a little medical assistance will be used. Out of the huge arsenal of instruments of torture available to the medical profession, those required for a ventouse extraction, and forceps, must rank right up at the top. They are both brutal-looking but highly effective; you might even consider stealing some just to frame them.

In the case of ventouse extraction, a metal or plastic cap is placed over the baby's head and a vacuum created by pumping air out through a hose. It really does look like a bicycle pump connected to a pigskin lampshade – but don't let that put you off! With some heavy tugs, the midwives and/or doctor will pull the baby out. Like forceps, they will also leave a tell-tale red mark on the baby's head and possibly even give your baby a cone-shaped head; don't worry, the marks and the egg-head will gradually fade away.

If ventouse extraction is not successful, then say hello to forceps. They actually look like a weird pair of barbeque tongs and the procedure is not dissimilar to that of removing a piece of toast that has become wedged in the toaster. Brings tears to your eyes, doesn't it? If used, they are likely to leave visible welts on the side of the child's head, but these too will disappear after a matter of days. One mum did reveal that, whilst she was not happy that forceps were being used, there was so much activity downstairs that it hardly seemed to matter if some forceps were making an appearance as well. At the end of the day her son was born healthy. Still, hardly a fun experience.

Assisted births are very common, accounting for as many as one in five. Despite the crude tools, they are the best that anyone has invented so far, and any side effects caused are not lasting.

Now That's Going To Hurt In The Morning!

Just when your partner thought she had endured it all in terms of pain and discomfort, an episiotomy may be necessary. An episiotomy is a surgical cut in the perineum, a particularly sensitive area between your partner's vagina and her back passage. Essentially the equivalent of the area from the back of your scrotum to your anus, and you know exactly how sensitive that is. An episiotomy is usually performed under local anaesthetic, but sometimes not. One will be done if the baby needs to be born quickly, because she is becoming distressed or if your partner is likely to tear badly. They are very common with forceps and ventouse deliveries. The incision is generally not all that painful for your partner (bearing in mind what else is going on at the time) but the healing process can be long and drawn out. An episiotomy will also affect how quickly you are both able to enjoy sex again after the birth.

Cutting The Cord

Now that baby has finally emerged it is time to partake in that age-old ritual, cutting the umbilical cord. If you wish to cut the cord you should put it on the birth plan, or you could just ask while you are there. Be sure to remind the midwife if you want to do this, even if it is written in capital letters and underlined in red, blue and black ink, as in all the excitement it can be overlooked. Cutting the cord does not hurt either the baby or mum, as there are no nerves involved (except maybe your own, and they are now completely shot!).

A salutary tale: about twenty minutes after Alia's arrival, I was sitting with her as Lisa was taking her shower. I mentioned to the midwife that I had wanted to cut the cord and she apologized for doing it automatically. She went on to say that it was a common joke at Hemel Hospital to give the father a blunt pair of scissors for the job. The combination of nerves, emotion and poor equipment made for some very amusing attempts by the fathers. Man, those midwives have a laugh!

The Third Stage Of Labour

Just when you think that it's all over, time to get your coat and spread the good news, your partner will be asked to push again. Somewhat confused, you may wish to remind the midwife that there's been enough pushing and grunting to last you a lifetime – can this woman not get enough of other people's agony? Can she not see the little bundle of joy that proves that the pushing phase has come to a natural and obvious conclusion?

I am afraid that the midwife (as always) is right. The final part of labour – the expulsion of the placenta, or after-birth – will mark the end of labour proper. Your partner may receive an injection to help her uterus close quickly, assisting with the expulsion. In extreme cases, the placenta may have to be removed by hand, which can be hugely upsetting to see, for you and your partner.

The placenta is a reddish/purple/green mess. It actually looks like something from *Aliens* and I was fascinated yet scared when it popped out. The midwife will usually collect the placenta on the bed between your partner's legs, to ensure that it is all present and correct.

It is edible, and they say incredibly nutritious. Probably more protein than a pint or two of Guinness and maybe even a 12-pack of mackerel – but after you have seen one, I defy anyone to put it anywhere near their mouth. You can request to take the placenta home with you, but I would strongly suggest you let the hospital deal with it; or better yet call in Ripley, Bishop and the rest of the team, armed with pulse rifles.

In Stitches

Your fascination with the bloody and gruesome aspects of birth may well continue if you choose to watch the stitching process. Stitching is required if there has been any tearing, or if an episiotomy was performed to aid the birth. One father described the carnage scene after the birth as like looking at a Jackson Pollock painting. Midwives and doctors are usually both competent and professional, and often set to work like master-seamstresses. Occasionally they do mess up and it can be excruciating for your partner if they are having trouble fixing the damage.

Don't make the big mistake I did of asking the midwife to

throw in a few extra stitches, 'You know, just for the sake of it,' which won me scowls and instant hatred from the three midwives and Lisa simultaneously. For a few minutes, you will be demoted from champion birth partner to scum of the earth. The midwife reminded me she knew what she was doing. I don't think that I will ever be on her Christmas card list. Lisa, fortunately, forgave me. Lesson 108: Do not make jokes about stitching.

The stitches will dissolve in a matter of weeks, so thankfully they do not need to be removed, unless they have been put in incorrectly in the first place. A local anaesthetic is employed to numb the area. Bearing in mind that your partner has just given birth and the whole area is feeling a tad sensitive right at that moment, this usually simple injection borders on being almost as bad as the birth. One mother wailed loudly enough for the whole hospital to hear: 'What fresh butchery are you performing on me now? I'll see you in court for this!' (Yes, it was Max's drama-queen wife again). However high most mothers will feel at the sight of their new-born child, any further tinkering downstairs is not going to be welcome.

Shower

It seems pretty cruel, so soon after the birth, for the midwife to insist that your partner stands up and takes a shower. If it were me, I would be too shaky to stand and too tired to care, but then again, during childbirth just about every bodily fluid other than earwax, makes an appearance at one stage or another. So rather than being covered in excrement, wee, saliva, mucus, snot, sweat, blood and vernix I would probably opt for a few minutes under a power shower too – make that twenty.

The walk from the bed to the shower is like some very good acting from a very bad 1950s horror flick. Understandably feeling a little delicate, your partner will take very short steps very slowly. This is easy to understand and you feel for her. Then you look down on the once-clean tiled floor and you see the trail of blood, and the bloody handprint she's left on the wall as she steadied herself. If you didn't pass out during the birth, you might want to now.

Your partner may recount afterwards that this shower is a difficult but necessary stage. The water will be refreshing and strangely soothing, although it might be pretty hard for her to put her paper maternity knickers on afterwards without getting them soaked, or without her falling over.

Meanwhile, *you* get to hold your baby and probably couldn't care less; in fact the longer she's in there, the better.

Holding Your Child For The First Time

It is the moment you long for as soon as you learn your partner is pregnant. No matter what your initial ambivalence, you always want to know what she will look like, what colour hair she will they have, what colour eyes? Will she look like me or like Mum? In fact, for nine months you wonder constantly about your child, and suddenly there she is, wrapped in a hospital blanket and being handed to you. The moment of truth is indescribable without using what can only be perceived as hyperbolic clichés. But I won't let that stop me, and nor will you.

The very first thought I had as I witnessed Alia come into the world was: 'Oh! It's a girl?' This wasn't disappointment, it was disbelief. In part, because I was absolutely 120 per cent sure that she was going to be a boy and in part because I could see a real, live, crying baby girl that was part of me; that I had helped create.

Holding your child for the first time allows you to see and understand your strengths and weaknesses as a human being. Holding her means that you can no longer act the eejit any more; you have responsibilities like never before. Holding her might make you think that you are nothing and she is everything. Holding your new-born baby is both terrifying and inspiring. Birth is one of the greatest paradoxes in life: having children is at once the most natural and ordinary thing in the world; yet at the same time incomparably profound and extraordinary. If you think the language seems exaggerated, wait until it happens to you. If you felt as if your life was missing something before the birth, you most certainly won't now.

You may well feel as if you are getting the lion's share of the baby-holding experience immediately after the birth; you will be able to hold her the whole time during the third stage of labour, the stitching and during the shower. In the case of a caesarean section this dad-time is increased. Although it is brief, in this time you will magically lose your fears about holding a child and how you will ever be able to stop them from crying. You'll even learn how to get up and sit down whilst holding her. Of course, fathers who have done all of the above laugh at how easy it is, but until we have tried I think we all wonder if we can cope.

Savour The Moment

Holding your child for the first time is an absolute delight and if either of you have the presence of mind to remember I would strongly suggest you get the other, or a midwife, to take a photo – there's very few times in life that you will have such a comparable grin.

I don't think any bloke can fully accept the reality of

becoming a father until the moment of actual birth. The whole planning of a pregnancy, the pregnancy itself, and even labour are stages where our interest grows as time progresses; but it is almost as if all these stages have absolutely nothing to do with becoming a father, ridiculous as it might sound. No matter how prepared you think you are, no matter how many hundreds of pages you have read in anticipation, nothing and nobody can explain how perfect seeing your child for the first time actually is.

Boys Don't Cry

Yes they do, a lot it seems, especially when a baby has just been born and you are the dad. If you haven't cried since you were twelve and the big boys from the sixth form tripped you up outside your geography class, the birth of your child is likely to bring the waterworks on, whether you like it or not. There is nothing wimpy or silly about a grown man crying at the sight, and relief, of a successful birth. Let it flow and feel free to sniffle. You will have the tissues ready in your pocket if you followed the advice in the last chapter. And you will never see the midwives again, at least not for nine months anyway, so no one's going to tell.

And That's A Wrap

Like dumbstruck lovers, or possibly just dumb lovers, you will just sit and stare at either your baby or your partner for countless minutes after the birth. What can you say after witnessing such an epic event? You will look up and notice that the rabble that were crowding the room during the birth have scampered off, to do it all again, in the next room. The conversation may be a little stifled, but who cares? Delivery Suite 4 doesn't look so bad now, mainly due to someone switching off the fluorescent lights and leaving you in almost complete darkness. With heavy eyes, you look from partner to baby and back to partner, and your cheeks might well be hurting now from the permanent grin that's been etched on your face since the birth.

You are alone: mum, dad and baby – all quiet, all tired and all very, very happy.

9. Immediate Aftermath

the end of
single life

A Night On The Ward

Unless your partner gave birth at home, mother and baby will most likely spend their first night together in the hospital's maternity ward. Don't be surprised if your first sight of this ward reminds you of some late-night movie you once watched about a labour camp in Siberia. Everyone, including the nurses nearing the end of their 43-hour shift, looks dishevelled, malnourished and close to collapse. Everyone is speaking in hushed tones, partly out of respect for others, but mainly because that's all they are capable of. Some of the other women will be fast asleep; many will be trying to handle the intricacies of breast feeding. The other new dads might look up to give you a nod; you respond in kind. There seems to be a mass of bedding everywhere but what will strike you most are the small fish-tank-like Perspex cots, each holding a new-born baby. Your baby will be put in one too, and your partner will be soon tucked up in a hospital bed next to it.

Sadly, all *you* will get is a well-worn chair that could probably benefit from the insertion of a folded beer mat under the left rear leg, not that there's likely to be many lying around. You're back to staring at your child in the cot, and mumbling something about escaping to Vladivostok when the revolution's over, just to keep in the spirit of your surroundings.

Bag Of (Forgotten) Tricks

It's a truth universally accepted, at least if you went to the antenatal classes or read your books, that you need a whole range of stuff with you at the time of delivery. You, like me, no doubt arrived at hospital with bags of goodies and equipment, in anticipation of a long labour and beyond. For many of you, once the contractions began, the bags and contents will be completely forgotten. It wasn't until Lisa was being wheeled to the maternity ward and begged me for a drink of water that I realized what was weighing me down. There I was, carrying litres of the stuff, along with sandwiches, soup, fruit and a global positioning system. Even during the longest labours I doubt many people think about tucking into a picnic. The bags will come home with you as heavy as when you went in, minus maybe a bottle of Volvic and a Double Decker.

I wouldn't advise against bringing your bags of goodies, but I would suggest that you think about the practicality of some of the stuff you are told to bring. I still wonder why I had a pair of shorts, flip-flops, underwear, and even slippers in my bag; bearing in mind it was November.

One thing I didn't bring, which would have brightened up Alia's incredibly boring perspex cot, was a small cuddly toy – I doubt Alia would have noticed, and I doubt even Lisa or I would have noticed, but thinking back it would have been nice to have personalized Alia's first bed with a little more than her name on her wristband.

Letting People Know

Although you might prefer to wait until you're back in the comfort of your own home, a few of us, myself included, couldn't help but leave the hospital briefly to make a few calls from the mobile phone. It was very early in the morning when this happened, but all the recipients concerned had specifically said 'Call as soon as you can.' So I did. It was with each phone call to family and friends that the reality of Alia and all that had just happened began to sink in. And it was the reality of 5.30 a.m. that made my relatives wish they had said 'Phone me as soon as it is a socially acceptable time.' Of course they all wanted details of the delivery and descriptions of Alia – unbelievably difficult to do when you're fighting exhaustion, myriad emotions and the harsh reality of a British winter after the womb-like ambience of a delivery suite.

I struggled for a few minutes with a ridiculously large cigar that I had brought with me for the purpose, but, even as a hardened smoker, I lost to the freezing November morning air and my anxiety to get back inside to see Lisa and Alia. I doubt I did those first conversations, or that cigar, much justice at all. With hindsight I should just have rang those closest to me, and asked them to share the news and probably bypassed the cigar altogether – you live and learn.

Pick-And-Mix Emotions

After the euphoria and overdose of adrenalin finally leaves your body a few hours after the birth, you will be exhausted – nowhere near in the same league as your partner, but exhausted nonetheless. Some fathers mentioned that that feeling of fatigue does not leave for at least the first year. In a way that is true, especially if your baby does not sleep through the night.

Others said that they felt strangely impotent in the first few days after the birth. Although the joy of seeing your baby born counteracts all of the negatives, some said they felt as if they'd been invited into the delivery suite simply on a sympathy ticket, as though it would be too upsetting to be asked to wait outside.

This feeling can continue in the very early days of your baby's life. Mother and baby will be very much wrapped up in each other, especially if your partner is breastfeeding. Remember that though you may feel at times like a glorified errand-boy – there to deliver chocolate and magazines, bring along clothes and toiletries, and administer back-rubs on demand – you are still playing a crucial role, and every second spent with mother and baby will help strengthen the bond of your new family.

Time Please, Gentlemen

Despite the garish-coloured curtains, there is very little privacy for patients on hospital wards. At some point you will be sent home to give your partner, the other patients and the nursing staff some room to get on with their respective roles – recovering and looking after those who are recovering. It is both distressing and annoying to be moved on, with the vivid images of birth still very much in the forefront of your mind. Your baby will be a matter of minutes, possibly hours old, and after waiting nine months to meet him or her, you have to take yourself off home. This is where home-birth fathers can laugh manically. However, you need your rest just as your partner does, so ultimately it is probably a blessing in disguise.

Our arrival on the maternity ward was unfortunately timed at about forty minutes before breakfast. I felt like I had hardly sat down when a nurse, as nicely as she could, asked me to leave the hospital and to come back in the afternoon. I could see that Lisa was exhausted and that Alia was already asleep, but it felt dreadful to leave them.

Home Alone

Dads with family and friends living close by would do well to meet up with them for a short while during the times that you are not at the hospital. When I got home I was incredibly tired but simply unable to sleep – I was totally wired on the experience. I made some additional calls to spread the good news and even managed to post some pictures of Alia up onto the Web, only a matter of five hours after she had been born. But there was something missing; well two things actually – Lisa and Alia. Frustratingly, my friends were at work and both my family and Lisa's were at opposite ends of the country. I wound up drinking far too much coffee and counting the minutes until it was time for afternoon visiting. Each hospital will have a different policy on visiting hours but the general rule is that they are never long enough for most new dads. I probably arrived at least forty minutes early, but no one seemed to mind.

You may, of course, just want to head back home, stick on

a film and crack open a cold beer for your own private celebration. The numbness is odd, a bit like the feeling you get when you have been awake all night (in many cases you have). Emotionally drained, yet charged. Exhausted, yet hyperactive.

Use this time out to look around your house, especially the lounge and the kitchen. No matter what state they are in, this will be the cleanest and emptiest they will be for the next 18 years!

Where's The Present?

This was my one big mistake. I didn't get into trouble for it but I was the only bloke in the entire ward (world?) not to give his partner a gift after the birth! Was there a guide- book out there that I was unaware of? Was this a commonly held custom, like presents at Christmas or wedding rings, that I didn't know about? Well, like an eejit, I went unarmed to see Lisa and Alia the next day. We both heard squeals of delight as 'eternity' rings were unwrapped, huge bouquets of flowers were fixed in vases and big fat cheques were revealed with promises of postnatal shopping trips. And then there was me – unshaven, rough as an old dog, and worst of all, offering no present. Mmmm. How to lose a friend and alienate the mother of your child in one stroke. Here I have to add that I had actually bought flowers,

but it was a particularly large bouquet and I thought it was daft to cart it into the hospital, only to carry it out again a few hours later – they were sitting handsomely in the toilet bowl at home as I couldn't find a vase big enough!

If I can give you one piece of advice it is this: Take A Present! Save yourself the feeling of utter failure! No matter how big or small, no matter how much you think 'I don't do things just because everyone else does,' you will be the only one on the ward, trust me.

Visitors

Many fathers interviewed complained of the number of visitors that arrived at the hospital. It is understandable that everyone wants to wish you well and see the new arrival, but equally it is a very tiring experience for mum and dad to have to recount (again!) the tale of delivery and hear how much the baby's ears are just like Uncle Albert's.

We didn't have any visitors, which in a weird way was also bad, when everyone else's area of the ward was brimming with well-wishers and other people's families. It would have been nice if our friends and relations could have made it to the hospital, but the distances involved were too great. Instead we were lucky to get a few days of 'us' time before the troops descended over the weekend. If you do receive visitors to the hospital it is very important that, in the nicest possible way, it is clear that they can't stay too long. As you are both still taking the whole situation in, it is not fair on either of you to have to keep up the grins, when all you really want to do is sleep, for a very long time ... Hang on, is that a baby I hear crying? That sleep might just have to wait, possibly for a couple of years.

Wetting The Baby's Head

This is an absolutely essential ritual for the new father but one that can be surprisingly complicated to arrange. The best time for the occasion is when your partner is still in hospital with the baby, but sadly this is also a time when you will probably be too exhausted to manage anything more alcoholic than a can of Shandy Bass. Once you do get to celebrate, you might find that your friends are more interested in having a few pints and a general catch-up than sharing with you the new-found joys and fears of fatherhood.

With everything else that you'll have to organize and worry about now, arranging any kind of social gathering is going to be the least of your priorities; it is probably best left in the capable hands of one of your friends to do the phoning around. As often happens with weddings, funerals and any other life-changing events, you may find it pretty hard to switch off and fully enjoy yourself, but it can be a great way to relax, and sure beats going mad with doubt and worry on your own in a very empty house.

It may be some time before you get the chance or the inclination to go out again, so take your opportunities while you can.

The Krypton Factor

Meanwhile, back in the hospital a number of tests will be performed on your baby, usually when he is only about a day old. These are not arduous and your baby is likely to pass, so there shouldn't be any reason to worry. The tests differ from hospital to hospital, but usually they include a sort of dexterity test, in which the doctor will (cruelly, I think) jerk his hands as if he was letting go of your baby, to check if he grabs the air to prevent the fall. The doctor may also shine a light into your baby's eyes and check that he grabs his finger. All quite simple and painless, but I am afraid it means that your child has now got a 100 percent pass record at exams, and you might expect the same from him in every exam from now on.

Coming Home

Parking at any time, anywhere in the UK, within reasonable walking distance of a hospital, is pretty difficult. On the day that you will be extracting your partner and baby from the bowels of the maternity ward, you will be lucky to find a space within a short taxi ride of the hospital. Then you will have to pay astronomical charges for the privilege. Remember to bring lots and lots of change. In the same way that it would be a nice idea if expectant couples were issued with a flashing pink light for use when dashing to the hospital for the birth, it would also be nice to receive a special, exclusive car park pass allowing you to park at least within sight of the hospital grounds for the one occasion that you are collecting your partner and baby. But as this scheme is yet to filter through to those in charge, park the car, pay the money and get walking.

I distinctly remember Lisa saying, as we walked out of the hospital ward with Alia strapped into her brand-new car seat: 'I can't believe they're just letting us walk out of here with a baby!' It seems most new parents feel exactly the same. And they're right. You don't have to fill in any forms, nobody makes any enquiries, and most surprisingly, in this cut-throat world we live in, you don't have to pay anyone anything! Granted, you will be escorted to the door by a nurse, but with a brisk wave, that is it – you are on your own, unleashed into the world with a matter-of-hours-old child in your care.

Precious Cargo

You will drive home with more care that day than you ever have or will again. Every other car, bird, plane in the sky, and possibly even pedestrian is a potential threat to your baby; it will probably take you an hour instead of the usual twenty minutes to get back home. I remember so clearly carrying Alia into the lounge, asleep in her seat. We put her down next to the sofa and just looked at her. Had she stayed asleep we would have sat there, mesmerized and in silence, forever.

Already your home is transformed. Your kitchen is full of unrecognizable contraptions and there will be a sterilizer steaming away, bottles of milk in the fridge, and a huge array of nappies, creams, pads, cotton wool, and talc. And suddenly all the hardware, clothing and toys have a purpose.

Time Quake

The first few days of your baby's life are likely to be quite hectic. Not for the baby, who will mainly sleep during the day, except to feed and cry a bit. No, it is the stream of visitors, family and friends, descending on you from all around the country to see the new-born infant. Although every one of your guests is more than welcome, (apart from the woman from two doors down – there's something funny about her), it can be an exhausting few days.

Time flies when you're having fun, and even more so when you have a new-born to look after. Although individual days (and more specifically nights, when having rudely awoken you three hours ago, your child still won't go back to sleep) may seem incredibly long, because you see so much of them; before you know it you are not talking about your child's age as a matter of days, but weeks and then even months. It is astonishing how fast the first year (and some would say years) go by, so enjoy those early days, no matter how tired you feel, because it will all be over so quickly.

From Proud Parents ...

In the first few days after the birth you will both feel a great sense of achievement and pride. The euphoria of becoming parents is a pretty powerful force. For the first three of four days all you will do is grin and run around the place ensuring that absolutely everything is just right for your baby. The house has never been tidier – certainly not when you've had anything to do with it anyway. Already your baby is a matter of days old, rather than a matter of hours. Visitors are still knocking on the door and flowers are still arriving. You're already a master of the nappy change and you laugh when you recall the time when you thought that bathing a baby was a more difficult procedure than open-heart surgery. You have both managed an hour or so sleep a night and yet remain feeling pretty good. (The novelty of sleepless nights will soon wear off.)

... To Baby Blues

Alas, all good things come to an end and before the week is out your partner may well go full circle and become a weeping wreck. This is almost certainly not postnatal depression but what is commonly called the 'Baby Blues'. These are not tears of joy, as I mistakenly assumed, but tears of sadness.

'But you have a beautiful baby in your arms? What possible reason have you got to cry?' you might ask. Lots and lots it seems.

The major reason for this sudden dip in her happiness is the sudden drop in hormones she will experience after the baby is born. Throughout the pregnancy her body was awash with hormones helping her to carry the child and feel good. But a couple of days after the birth these hormones stop being produced, and now her body is going through a sort of withdrawal, or cold-turkey phase. Add to this that she is now finally starting to relax after the whirlwind of the previous few days, although she won't yet have fully recovered from the labour and birth. Many women, especially those who had to endure an episiotomy and/or stitching, can barely sit down for a good while after the birth, and those who have had Caesarean sections will have their own versions of pain and discomfort.

So far, it has been pure adrenalin and love of the new baby that has given her the strength and will to keep going. When exhaustion catches up, it will pole-axe your partner and it is not a pleasant sight. Worry not. The Baby Blues are, for most women, temporary. They may go through a few days of fear about their ability, their 'right', even their suitability to be a mother. As far as you will be concerned, from what you've seen so far your partner is possibly the most capable mother on the planet. She didn't feel awkward about changing nappies, or feeding the baby, like you did. How can she be questioning her ability? No one else is – not even your own mother! However, sometimes the Baby Blues do not disappear after a few days; sometimes they're here to stay for a while. If this is the case then she might be suffering from postnatal depression. If you are worried about her and feel that outside help may be required, then there is more about this in Chapter 11, under When Things Don't Go According To Plan, along with contact details in Chapter 12.

What Can You Do?

Support, Support, Support. You might well be feeling that you are in need of some support yourself, and that with the new baby on the scene you have become second in line in your partner's feelings and affections. But getting in a huff about being demoted from favourite to second best is really not going to help the situation. The stark truth is that in these early days you have to come second. You can look after yourself, the baby can't. Caring for both the baby and your partner really is the best way to feeling better about yourself.

Will You Cope?

The answer is, quite simply, yes, of course you will. But, even if during the entire process of your partner's pregnancy you were on top of things emotionally, I suspect that now your child is home with you, you may begin to have your doubts. For the entire nine months of pregnancy you and your partner were preparing yourselves for the baby to arrive. Despite this, when he or she is actually home with you, it is exactly how you imagined yet completely different. Some fathers admitted that their early fears about responsibility, finances and inexperience came flooding back, only this time worse than ever before. Despite their elation at becoming a dad (sometimes again) they were bowled over by actually seeing a baby in the car seat, in the Moses basket, or sucking from a breast or a bottle.

The pushchair that had been waiting patiently under the stairs or in the garage now has slightly worn wheels. The soft white blankets, so neatly folded for so many weeks, are strewn around the house, or in a wash basket about to endure the first of many, many washes. It is all suddenly very real and very exciting. Then a moment of clarity – you realize that you won't just cope, you'll be pretty good at it too, and dare I say, might even enjoy it!

Midwife Visits

If you do ever feel that you aren't on top of things, there is a strong support system for new parents. Part of the postnatal care currently offered in the UK involves a series of visits from your midwife in the first week or two to check that baby is settling in and mum and dad are coping. This midwife will probably be the one that your partner saw throughout the last stages of pregnancy, or when she was giving birth. She will show you all the essentials with regard to nappies, baths and breastfeeding. She will weigh your child and ask you how you are both feeling. Be honest with her if you're feeling pretty dreadful – it really helps to talk things through and believe me, she's heard it all before.

As the days go by, the visits become less frequent, and by the end of the second week you will both probably feel like you have been doing it all for years.

Coming To Terms With Fatherhood

For many it happens when you first see your child. That moment, whether it is in the delivery suite or somewhere else, is quite frankly monumental. You are a dad.

I am not very good at visibly expressing my emotions, but I have to say that seeing Alia literally 'pop' out and let out her first sound was the closest this man has come to openly weeping since I was ten years old and my brother kicked me in the goolies. I underwent a complete mixture of emotions, each fighting for my brain's attention – excitement, fear, nervousness, happiness, fulfilment, pride. I had created a mini-me. The moment my eyes saw her, I made an unspoken pact with my daughter – to love, serve and protect her forever. But had I come to terms with fatherhood, now that I was a father? Not immediately.

Some fathers come to terms with fatherhood during the pregnancy and some many years into their child's life. I fell somewhere in between: I recognized that I was a father straight away, but fatherhood and all that it entailed probably didn't really sink in until a few weeks after Alia's birth. Bonding with your child is not always immediate. It tends to take us a bit of time, and with the focus on the relationship between mother and baby it's almost as if there's no room for you. For some dads true bonding happens once their baby smiles at them, for others it's a lot later on in the child's development. The important thing is to be patient, with yourself, and your baby – don't worry if you feel a little bit detached; you both need to get used to each other, and by simply spending time together this will be easily achieved.

Well Done, Dad!

No one ever remembers to say well done to the dad, so I'm going to: well done to you all. I bet you feel a bit of a divvy now. All that worry, and all that angst. It was easy, wasn't it? You thought it was a nuclear winter that was on its way, not an eight-pound-something child with a nose you can't help but fawn over and a funny bottom lip that quivers all the time.

The pregnancy is over, the birth was actually enjoyable and there, sitting (or more accurately, lying down fast asleep) on the floor, is a tiny baby – perfectly content with his or her surroundings, despite the fact that you never got round to putting the blinds up, or applying another coat of paint to the skirting boards. You're only days into officially being a dad, but already the path is etched out, the coast is clear, and, for the first time in nigh on a year, you actually feel in control of the situation. Whilst very much not in command, you certainly feel you are a very close, favoured, lieutenant.

The adventure has only just begun. Do what feels right – because it probably will be right. There are no hard- and-fast rules about how to cope with a new-born baby – your baby. Don't be shy, have a go at everything, and most importantly enjoy every last minute.

10. Father, Mother & Baby Are Doing Fine

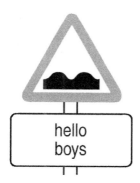

hello
boys

Just A State Of Mind

The elation lasts for weeks. No matter how little sleep you've had, no matter how many nappies you've changed, no matter how many times you have wanted to collapse with nervous and physical exhaustion, your baby will coo at you, just once, and nothing else matters. However, you do also need to get your head around the basics, fast. In a way, you will almost be as much on show as your baby. So here are a few tips to get you off to a flying start.

Breast Or Bottle – The Great Debate

Just as there are two opposing camps regarding the use of pain relief in labour, you will quickly learn that there are two camps regarding breastfeeding. The difference is that this will probably be a decision reached through experience, rather than belief. Almost all women will attempt to breast- feed their child. Certainly, whilst in hospital they will be positively encouraged to do so, and will probably face a stern look of disappointment from the midwives and nurses if they don't at least give it a go.

It is instinctive and natural, and by the time of the birth it is likely that your partner's breasts will be aching to lactate, and quite possibly leaking to prove the point. And yes, it is undeniable that breast is best. Not only will your baby be getting all the food she needs, at exactly the right temperature, without any artificial additives, she will also be absorbing vital immunities from the mother, which help protect against all manner of childhood illnesses and ailments. No matter how sophisticated bottle milk becomes, it is never going to be able to mimic that protection because of the unique match that breast milk has between mother and baby.

It May Be Natural But It's Not Always Easy

However, no matter how much your partner wants to breastfeed it might not always be possible. It is initially a very tricky manoeuvre for mum to correctly dock your baby's mouth, and some babies have problems getting to grips with the procedure too. One father described how his partner was having real problems with feeding in the early days because the baby wasn't 'latching on' properly. But she was uncomfortably full of milk – I think 'engorged' is an appropriate term. He came home early from work one day to find her sitting on a stool with her top down, a tortuous- looking breast pump sucking away at one nipple and her friendly neighbourhood midwife at the other, manually squeezing the milk out into a cup.

Tears were streaming down the poor woman's face, probably due as much to the indignity of it all as to the pain.

Added to that, the baby's ferocious sucking can often lead to sores and even scabs forming on the nipples, which have been described as simply unbearable. You can be of some assistance here. It is actually quite difficult at first, for many women, to get your baby to latch on. Us blokes tend not to be too shy when it comes to man handling our partner's breasts – now's your opportunity to grab for a good reason. Your extra pair of hands will be a great help in ensuring that baby's mouth 'docks' correctly and the milk can flow. Be aware that some babies are remarkably hungry and the frustration of a crying new-born coupled with the agony of sore breasts often leads to resignation from the breastfeeding camp and reliance on formula milk.

Your partner's breast size has nothing to do with the amount of milk that she will be able to produce. Whilst they do store, and leak, a reservoir of milk because her body is always producing the stuff, it is the sucking action of the baby that stimulates the pituitary gland, thus releasing a hormone that demands more milk is produced. For an amusing laugh (although the joke will wear very thin, very quickly, for your partner) mimic the sucking noise of your child to cause a squirt of milk. For maximum effect, do this on your first evening out without baby, when she is wearing her best slinky new top and has forgotten to put the nursing pads in her bra. On the other hand, being with her in public view with two huge wet circles at her breasts could be a little embarrassing for you, too.

Finally, albeit a little bizarre, the antibodies found in breast milk can be effective externally as well as when they are ingested. A case in point: Alia awoke one morning with her eyes glued together with mucus. Lisa expressed some milk and dabbed it in Alia's eyes. Not only did the milk help loosen the now solid mucus, application of milk throughout the day also cleared up the infection and by the following morning there was no trace of a problem at all.

Support Her Decision

Whichever method suits your partner will be the one that you, and she, learn to believe strongly in. The breast feeders can't understand why formula feeders caved in under the pain. They enjoy the bonding that breastfeeding allows and nothing feels more natural. The formula feeders can feel frustrated, and even that they have 'failed' in some way because they were not able to breastfeed. On the plus side, they argue that formula milk is heavier, allowing baby to sleep better and generally be more content.

I could have imagined it, but I think there is some rivalry going on between breast and bottle-feeders. Whilst breastfeeding is of course nature's way, bottle-feeding does serve the same purpose. As to whether one is better than the other, apart from the lack of antibodies in formula milk there is not an awful lot of difference. Except, of course, the outrageous cost of formula.

Whichever route your partner decides upon will lead to the same result; your child will feel full for about three hours and then she will feed again. At least if your baby is bottle fed, *you* will have an opportunity to feed her too. Support your partner's decision whatever it may be – your child is being fed and that's all that really matters.

Feed me, Seymour, Feed Me

If your partner is breastfeeding, then you can probably avoid this section because you are unlikely to need to know anything about bottle-feeding, other than the steep cost of the bottles and sterilizer that you went and bought anyway. Go on, take a look at them, sitting there idle in the kitchen, possibly with the price tag still attached.

If your partner has chosen to breastfeed then, for about four months, whenever your baby hollers at you because she is hungry, you simply holler in turn to your partner, 'Milk Machine'. Reluctantly, but very promptly, a breast will be whipped out and within milliseconds your baby will be as content as can be, sucking furiously at the very life juice that will sustain her. It is a magnificent sight and one of those few occasions when life is worth living just for that experience.

Alternatively, if breastfeeding is not the chosen option in your household, you will need to become familiar with formula milk. 'What do you mean "Milk Machine"? I gave up breastfeeding two months ago. Maybe it's about time *you* went and fixed the twins a bottle?'

Making up a bottle is straightforward. You match the number of ounces of water with the same number of scoops. For most babies you will be making five ounces of milk per feed. For hungrier babies you might just want to find a pint glass, or better yet a bucket. Alternatively you can buy formula pre-mixed in a carton, but this can prove costly.

The most important thing is the temperature you serve the milk at. Ideally, you want to be mimicking your partner's body temperature, and so you will need to serve the milk warm, not cold, and certainly not hot. Your next decision is whether to bring the milk up or down to temperature. You have the choice of making the milk with boiled (but now cool) water and placing the bottle in a saucepan or bowl of boiling water (or microwave), thus gradually warming it up. Or, you can make it with boiling water and then wait for it to cool down. The intensity of your baby's screaming will quickly determine which method is best suited for the occasion, the long and the short of it is find the fastest possible.

You Could Tarmac A Road With That

Your child's first poo, which will probably make an appearance a day or two after she comes out of hospital, is a sight to behold. Fathers I spoke to used every colour of the rainbow to describe it over the course of the interviews. Usually it's a sort of black-green combination, gelatinous in consistency, and a bugger to clean off her legs and bottom. The stuff is like glue.

Meconium, as it is known, is the net result of nine months' build-up of dead cells, amniotic fluid (the same stuff that probably had your baby hiccupping in the womb), bile and mucus. Although it is a half-hour exercise (exorcise?) to clean the stuff up, its appearance is a sure sign that your baby's bowels are in tip-top shape. Your partner's health visitor or midwife will ask your partner to confirm that it has been passed.

The dark black or green colour will go. After a few days your baby's poo will just be waste from the breast or bottle milk. Expect to see more delicate shades of brown and green for the next few weeks. Yes, they do smell, but nowhere near as bad as yours; that is, until they move on to solid food.

Spotify Dad

'When you get a moment listening to thousands of tracks on the Internet, could you come and deal with your child's arse, please?'

It was the bit that you weren't looking forward to. But the moment has now arrived. I still think that it would have been far more useful at the antenatal classes if, rather than sitting on a crumb-ridden carpet inhaling the scent of Eric and company's week-old socks, we had been allowed to practice changing a nappy on a child's doll. Granted, the midwife, when she comes to visit, will show you how to change a nappy but the proof is in the pudding, and although you love your baby you certainly don't want any of that black stuff anywhere near your hands or fingernails.

I knelt on the floor and placed Alia carefully in front of me. There she was, blissfully cooing away on the changing mat. I, on the other hand, was having palpitations and running a bit of a sweat. I had the new nappy, the lukewarm water, the talc and the creams to my right, and an industrial bag of cotton wool balls to my left. I tore at the nappy and eventually the sticky bits gave in to pressure and opened. Poo everywhere. Oh no, it's all over her bits and her legs, not a bit anywhere near her actual bum how did that happen? The cleaning bit is relatively easy, unless you drench the cotton wool, which tends to spread the poo about rather than cleaning it up, thus prolonging the agony.

Finally she's clean and I am ready to apply my first nappy. I pull on the tabs – no sticky! I reach for the bag of nappies, take out the next one and pull on the tabs – again, no sticky! What's going on? I repeat the process about ten times and get more and furious with one of the biggest nappy manufacturers in the UK, and with myself for falling at the last hurdle. Beaten, I shout for Lisa. It turns out that there *was* sticky, I had just been pulling at the wrong bit of the tab, exposing the 'dry' side rather than the sticky side. So after destroying an entire pack of nappies it was done
… Who says men are useless?

Nappies are, in fact, a doddle. By the end of week one, you may have changed so many that you will feel as if you have been doing it for years. Time yourself. My personal best (for a poo, not a wee) was 16 seconds.

Crying

'What's that, sweetheart? Did you just ask if it would be alright to have a small bottle of milk, followed by a cuddle and a gentle rock, topped off with a light snooze, before a brisk walk in the park?' Well, actually it was more like, 'Waaaaaaaaaaaagh.' Breath. 'Waaaaaaaaaaaaaaaaagh.' Breath. Repeat.

Your baby will cry and cry and cry. Usually whenever you and your partner are trying to catch a bit of shut-eye yourselves. Crying is the only means of communication currently open to your child. Don't worry, it only lasts for about a year, by which stage your baby will be able to call the emergency services all by herself, whilst turning on the video you thought was successfully hidden under the sofa. Unable to do anything for themselves, babies rely on someone else (namely you and the missus) to provide them with the food, warmth and comfort that they need. Crying is a baby's way of communicating one or all of those needs. Within a few weeks you will begin to notice alterations in the tone and pitch of the cry that usually (but not always) gives you a clue to what the request is for. Crying generally indicates the following:

Hunger

This one's easy to deal with. If she's breastfed, you pass the baby across to your partner and return to reading the sports pages. If bottle-fed, retrieve 'here's one I prepared earlier' from the fridge, heat, test and apply to baby's mouth. Although hunger may not be the root cause of the crying, for the duration of the feed peace is returned to your home. This peace may be followed rather quickly by more crying, which could mean:

Nappy

Much as *you* would probably not enjoy festering in your own excrement, babies aren't too hot on the feeling either. As babies become toddlers there is no escaping the smell of poo and you react accordingly. However, young baby's poo does not always smell enough to escape the nappy and therefore it is wise to have a quick peek to see if this could be why your baby is still crying. But what if the nappies all changed, but still she continues?

Ambience

Funnily enough it might be the act of changing the nappy that replaces one concern with another. Having only experienced the claustrophobic enclosures of a womb since conception, external atmospheres can play havoc on a baby's senses. The air is much cooler now that they are stripped off, and it's not nice. As well as trying to beat my record of 16 seconds, you will probably want to speed up nappy changes to cause as little distress as possible to your baby.

The sensitivity to temperature goes for when your baby is in her cot or basket too. Apply layers of clothes and bedding rather than heaping all your hopes on a single heavy blanket or duvet. With layers it is much easier to help your baby warm up or cool down ever so slightly. Many babies also like to be 'swaddled' in their blankets, thus recreating a womb-like feeling. (Some adults might admit to quite liking this too ...

Cuddles

Babies might only weigh less than ten pounds, but standing up with them for hours can be exhausting, and nerve-racking, until you get used to holding a baby properly. Babies love being held, and in the early weeks being rocked or swayed is incredibly reminiscent of life in the womb, and will usually result in sleep. Alia seemed particularly happy sleeping on my chest, and on waking would attempt to seek out my nipple for a quick feed.

Use a cushion to support your arm, if you have the baby with you on the sofa; it stops you getting a painful ache. A couple of fathers even coyly admitted that sitting with their sleeping baby in their arms was one of the nicest feelings they'd experienced in a long while. They preferred me not to mention them by name.

Pain

Birth is a traumatic experience for both your partner and your baby. Your baby might cry because it simply preferred the peaceful environment of mummy's tummy to the noisy real world. To use a music analogy, it must be like someone removing you from a room full of soft cushions, sweet incense and the gentle music of The Orb, and dumping you unceremoniously in the front row of a Metallica gig.

Also, about one in five babies develop colic, which is a yet-to-be explained phenomenon that most medical practitioners associate with your baby's digestive tract not quite coping with the sudden introduction of milk. There is no proven cure for colic, although there are plenty of things you can try. Thankfully, it does not have any long-term effects. It is incredibly hard to hear a baby cry for hours on end, without being able to help, but it does pass.

Stop Fussing

Ironically, too much fussing, cuddling, nappy changes, kisses and rocking can over-stimulate a baby. If this is the case she will actually be crying because you are doing too much, when really she just wants to be left in her basket staring fixatedly at the 100-watt bulb in the lounge. Of course, leaving her alone is the last thing you want to do, when she is crying, and therefore it is always the last thing you actually do. When the crying stops, you and your partner breathe a sigh of relief and having wasted half an hour going through this list, you wish you had left her a moment longer, before charging in with the cavalry. So the two of you promise that next time she starts crying you will leave her a while to calm down. All the best-laid plans go to waste, because the moment she starts crying you will repeat the whole process all over again.

And that's probably about it! You're now armed with at least the rudiments and ready to take on the challenge of looking after a new-born baby. It will be trying at times and intensely rewarding at others and it will all be a whole lot easier if you keep your wits and your sense of humour about you. Babies can be the most challenging and amusing little creatures. Enjoy your child, continue to enjoy your partner, and enjoy all the joys of fatherhood.

Section Two

11. When Things Don't Go To Plan

too much
responsibility

Postnatal Depression

I don't want to make light of it, but I found the best way to try to get an insight into postnatal depression is to look back to when you first learnt that your partner was pregnant. For those days, weeks or even the whole nine months, you had Post-Positive Test Result Depression. All those worries about your job, money, time and ability to cope hit you nine months before they did your partner. You've recovered, and now the baby is there in the flesh and you're just getting on with it all. For your partner, however, those fears are very much in the now and, more importantly, may be magnified 100 times over.

For about one in every ten mothers, this feeling of inadequacy and inability to cope lasts much longer than those fabled few 'Baby Blues' days. Days can become weeks and even months. It is important to realize that postnatal depression is a serious illness, and if not recognized or treated can develop, in severe cases, into full psychosis, a state which is disastrous for both mother and baby. Fortunately, if it is correctly diagnosed, it can be cured. There are some tell-tale symptoms which separate the Baby Blues from proper postnatal depression that you can be on the lookout for:

Feeling Very Low And Worthless

This is the most common symptom and I suppose the most obvious. Your partner will be feeling very low about herself and even about being a mother, and this feeling does not abate. Often the depression comes in phases, possibly triggered by certain times of the day, but sometimes it is completely unpredictable. Previous sufferers described it as intense sadness, being miserable and feeling incredibly lonely, even though they had a small baby constantly by their side. Your partner may be unwilling to make commitments too far in advance (like next Tuesday), and will seem very isolated from friends, other mothers and you.

Extreme Fatigue

You will be used to seeing your partner exhausted from about the start of the third trimester. You are also pretty tired now, what with all the night-time feeds, nappy changes and crying. There's also the small matter of somehow trying to concentrate on a full-time career, but I wouldn't advise complaining too much about that, as it is likely your partner is envious of your freedom to leave the house and the baby every day. But if your partner still seems extremely tired, day and night, even when she has help or the baby is sleeping a little better, this could be another symptom of depression.

Unable To sleep

So tired that she nods off with the baby for five minutes on the sofa, but so tired that she cannot sleep properly in a bed. Your partner may be feeling so depressed or worried about your baby that even though she wants and needs nothing more than good rest, she cannot get to sleep.

Irritability

The tell-tale sign for most dads that there may be something wrong with your partner is the intense irritability. Ironically, *you* may be the cause of it and you will be left wondering what you said or did wrong. Your partner may also be irritated with the baby, or breastfeeding, and once again it is likely that you, or maybe other children in the house, will get the brunt of it.

Lack Of Appetite

Her body is craving for nutrients and calories to help recover from the birth, and if she is breastfeeding she also needs to keep your baby healthy; but she might eat hardly anything at all, or, just as bad, eats lots of the wrong things. You might not be able to influence what gets eaten or not eaten during the day, but, much like during the latter part of pregnancy, it might be time to release the chef in you for the evening meal.

Can't Cope, Won't Cope

Your partner might be complaining that it is all too much, or breaking down on the telephone to you, or her friends, about the demands of the baby. She is anxious that the baby is not developing properly or that she is an unfit mother. The care of the baby is a chore, and an unwelcome one at that. The baby is never satisfied or ungrateful of her efforts. Your partner becomes overly concerned about your baby's health and runs to the doctor almost daily. Is the baby getting enough milk or maybe too much? Molehills have become mountains, and you're being shouted at for not worrying enough.

No One Is Immune

No matter how robust your partner's previous mental disposition, the Baby Blues and even postnatal depression can affect the 'strongest' of women. They will eventually go, but recognizing it and getting your partner to recognize it could save you both maybe months or years of suffering and unwelcome strains on your relationship as a couple. The best you can do is support and care for her as much as is humanly possible, and try to make sure she gets plenty of support from friends, family and the medical profession too. Now is not a time to try to do it alone.

Miscarriage

Miscarriage, or spontaneous abortion as it is referred to in medical circles, is unfortunately a common occurrence. There are no medical procedures that can reverse the situation once a miscarriage occurs. In the majority of cases, it is unusual for a doctor to give a medical reason for the cause of the miscarriage. Some medical journals claim that up to one in five of all pregnancies end in miscarriage. If this happens to you it can be devastating for both partners.

In many cases a miscarriage is preceded with bleeding, and this can last days or even weeks. However, some bleeding is common during the early weeks of pregnancy and does not always mean the pregnancy will end in miscarriage. Often the woman experiences cramping, which can be intense. All miscarriages are painful, both physically and emotionally. Some believe that for a childless couple the pain is worse; others say it is worse when you already have a child because you know more about what you are losing.

What Caused It?
Although hospitals and doctors operate differently, it is likely that until three 'official' miscarriages have occurred, neither partner will be asked to have tests. For a miscarriage to be 'official', then the pregnancy itself must be registered. Many women miscarry before they even know they are pregnant, or before they have alerted their doctor to the fact. There is an old wives' tale that you should not announce a pregnancy until after the first twelve weeks – essentially, after three months. There is some straightforward reasoning to this. Most miscarriages occur within these first three months: the less people that know of the pregnancy the less people have to be informed about the miscarriage
– always a painful and awkward process.

It is entirely your choice as a couple when you should tell the world that you are having a baby. Pregnancy is a joyous occasion, and if you are anything like me you'll have a beaming grin that gives the game away to even the most hardened of friends. Nevertheless, a little caution should be employed. By all means tell immediate family and close friends, but involving, say, work colleagues should probably wait until after this three-month 'talk embargo'. There really is nothing worse than the awkward scenario of someone whose name you hardly even know, plying sympathy on you after a miscarriage. Not that what they say is cruel or unsympathetic, in fact it's quite the opposite. What hurts the most about a miscarriage, for both the man and woman in the relationship, is the inevitable feeling of guilt and failure. The fact that Dave from Accounts feels the need to say 'I'm sorry about your loss' hurts more because Dave *is* sorry – whoever Dave is. My advice is to hold back the urge to tell until your partner becomes too obviously pregnant to hide the fact any longer. I do believe that, in the long run, it is easier for all concerned.

Assigning Blame

We all look for something or someone to blame when anything goes wrong in our lives, but on this occasion there really isn't any point. No one is to blame when a miscarriage occurs. Not you and certainly not your partner. Sadly, most people experiencing a miscarriage will look back and start finding fault with their actions or the actions of their partner over the previous few weeks and try to find correlations between the miscarriage and a particularly heated argument, or that athletic night in the bedroom, or the third glass of wine ... none of those activities lead to miscarriage and this really is a futile and counterproductive exercise.

Try to accept that what has happened has been for a reason – many doctors argue that a miscarriage is the body's natural way of ending a pregnancy that wasn't quite right from the start.

D&C

Depending on where, when, and at what stage of the pregnancy a miscarriage takes place, if there is even the smallest chance that not all of the foetus was expelled, then your partner might be required to undergo a dilatation and curettage evacuation. The operation is performed to reduce the chance of infection and ensure that your partner does not continue bleeding. It is a safe but unpleasant process that can be very emotional for both of you. Despite popular misconception (no pun intended), the D&C does not weaken your partner's cervix, reduce her chance of conceiving again, or make her more likely to miscarry in subsequent pregnancies.

Is History Repeating Itself?

As mentioned, miscarriage is shockingly common. This must be society's best-kept secret. When asked why I was writing a book about pregnancy, I would recount to those I felt comfortable with our experience in 2002, when Lisa and I suffered three miscarriages. So many people shared similar stories with me that I was amazed at how common miscarriage is and how well most people seem to cope. Unfortunately, many women miscarry more than once in their life. Officially, about one in thirty-six women will have two miscarriages due to nothing more than chance.

Should You Try Again?

Some couples decide that they want to begin trying again for a pregnancy right away, while others feel that it's too soon and that they need time to get over this loss. I have fallen, on different occasions, into both categories. In one respect, trying for another baby is both a bonding experience and a form of catharsis. After the first two miscarriages Lisa and I were determined we could help the healing process along by immediately trying again. By the time we had the third miscarriage, I, and especially Lisa, had become emotionally and physically drained and we agreed that a rest was the best course of action. There is no 'right' answer, and if there is ever a time to trust your instincts then it is now. Whatever you decide it will be the right decision. Medical circles will recommend a brief 'rest' interval before trying again, and certainly that your partner waits for her first period. There is a higher risk of miscarriage associated with pregnancies that occur if the pregnancy immediately follows a miscarriage without one menstrual cycle intervening, but then again, many successful pregnancies have started in this manner!

How Can We Improve Our Chances For Next Time?

As most miscarriages are caused by reasons beyond anyone's control, the simple answer is very little. However, there are changes that you can both make to your lifestyle that might assist fertility, and therefore a miscarriage could be the catalyst to a healthier lifestyle – for both partners. This of course starts with a regular exercise schedule if you do not have one already. A healthy diet, losing any excess pounds and cutting down on alcohol all help your chances of getting your partner pregnant again.

Premature Birth

A premature baby is one born before 37 weeks. It can be very worrying to find out that your partner is going to give birth prematurely, especially if you were both unaware it was a possibility and consequently unprepared. Many premature babies are delivered by caesarean section but some are still delivered vaginally; this is a decision taken by your midwife or doctor. There are many reasons for premature births, and it is almost a standard in the case of multiple births. Usually, your baby will be taken to the neonatal unit or intensive care unit of the hospital – allowing your baby to receive only the best care available.

The technology surrounding a baby born prematurely can be intimidating to you and your partner. All of the machinery is helping your baby survive – by regulating her breathing, her food and her temperature. Technology, and specialist care for premature babies, has moved on so much that, even compared to twenty years ago, a premature birth tends not to lead to ongoing problems for your child. Most parents of premature babies have nothing but praise for their hospital's special premature-care units. They tend to be the best-equipped and best-staffed areas of the hospital, because when it comes to making sure that a tiny life has the best possible chance available, everyone is on your side.

Baby In An Incubator

Those fathers interviewed whose babies were born prematurely all mentioned a feeling of impotence at watching their tiny babies in incubators. Your role as a father is not lessened because your baby is born prematurely; whilst you might not have the same opportunity to kiss and cuddle your baby, the love is no less strong, and in a matter of weeks the chances are that you will be at home changing nappies and getting no sleep. There are a number of organisations that can assist parents who experience premature births, miscarriages, abnormalities and stillbirths; their contact details are listed in Chapter 12.

Discovering Abnormalities

It has got to be the one thing that we worry about the most, on learning that our partner is pregnant. Will everything be okay? Will our child be 'normal'? If there is a problem, you may become aware of it at the first scan, or you may not discover it until the baby is actually born. It is at the ultrasound scan that essential measurements are taken, and most couples, are given the nod to say that baby is healthy and no abnormalities are evident at this stage.

The parameters for a 'healthy' child, many believe, are set a little narrow. Thus, the parameters for a baby being 'unhealthy' are particularly wide. Partly due to the blame culture of the West and the era of dial-a-lawsuit, doctors, hospitals and midwives now live and work in absolute dread of being sued for malpractice. 'Why didn't you tell me there was a chance that my baby might have Down's syndrome?' In response, if there is even the slightest, most infinitesimally small, chance of your baby being in anyway 'abnormal' then they will tell you. You will be invited back, usually to see a consultant soon after the scan, and, depending on the findings, he or she will talk you through some options. Put starkly, this will be to ask whether you want to continue with the pregnancy or not.

What Will You Do?

There are arguments for and against voluntary abortion, and there are many books and organizations that will furnish you with information and arguments for and against, far more eloquently than I can. I do not subscribe to any organized religion, but realize that many readers do. Mentioning abortion in this book is not an attempt to anger or fuel argument; just as there is a lack of information regarding spontaneous abortion (miscarriage) and pregnancy, there is, in my opinion, even less information about abortion, specifically for men. It is for this reason the topic cannot be ignored.

How you and your partner react to the news that there might be complications with the pregnancy is something that only the two of you can answer. I must stress that there have been thousands of cases, across the world, were a couple were warned that there was a problem and the arrival of a healthy baby proved the experts all wrong. This exact scenario happened to some good friends of ours and, thanks to their decision to continue with the pregnancy against all advice, there is now a beautiful, perfectly healthy three-year-old alive today. The medical establishment is not infallible.

One father interviewed, who did not want to be named, was warned that their baby would be born with a number of birth defects. The abnormalities were all physical; there was nothing that would affect the child's mental abilities. These disabilities included a cleft palate, club-foot, webbed toes, stomach problems and an abnormal left earlobe. The baby was born and after a series of minor operations is growing up to be a perfectly healthy and happy child.

Another couple interviewed had a much sadder experience. They were already about five months into the pregnancy when blood tests revealed that there was a very high risk of their baby having severe Down's syndrome. They were brought into the hospital and asked to think very carefully about their choices. They both stressed that everyone in the hospital was fantastic, very supportive and understanding, but they could tell that those involved were sure that the best option would be to end the pregnancy. Apparently, there was also a high risk that the pregnancy would spontaneously abort later on anyway, which would have been physically debilitating as well as incredibly harrowing.

Furthermore, if the baby did make it to full term it probably would not live long after being born.

Faced with such painful options, and having to make a decision very quickly, they decided to end the pregnancy. They both said that it was the hardest decision they had ever had to make. On top of that, the woman had to endure labour to deliver the baby as the pregnancy was too far advanced for a normal abortion. The whole experience left them absolutely devastated for months afterwards. Some things that helped heal the wound were giving the baby, a name, and giving him a proper funeral service where they could say goodbye. This is a tragic story but does have a happy endnote – the couple went on to have a perfectly normal pregnancy quite soon afterwards, and now have a beautiful, healthy one-year-old son.

Get As Much Support As You Can

Unfortunately I didn't get to talk to any couples who had children with genetic disabilities, but I'm sure if I had they would have shared with me mainly positive experiences. Many say that Down's syndrome babies are the most loved and the most loving of children – after all, they remain like innocent children in heart and mind all their lives.

Whatever your decision, if you are faced with this eventuality there are a number of organizations you can contact, details of which I have listed in Chapter 12. These people are trained to talk to you about all aspects of pregnancy and abortion. If you have any doubt whatsoever, please consult some of these people first, preferably with your partner. It's a chat that could change lives, quite literally.

Stillbirth

A stillbirth has got to be the most devastating thing that can happen to an expecting couple. Having carried a pregnancy for months; possibly having prepared the child's room, the child's toys and clothes, and even chosen names, this is the most awful of blows to endure. Surprisingly, 1 in 200 pregnancies result in a stillborn baby. Because many stillbirths occur in what appear to be normal pregnancies, the parents-to-be are rarely prepared for this utterly devastating outcome. In most cases, the specific cause of stillbirth is unknown. There are a number of causes directly attributed to stillbirth. Some of these are problems with the umbilical cord, birth defects, or placenta and maternal conditions existing before or developing during pregnancy. It is important to note that, while stillbirth is emotionally traumatic, most women will be able to conceive and carry a healthy baby, full term, in their next pregnancy. If the still- birth was caused by an umbilical cord problem, the chances of this repeating are minimal. If the cause was due to a maternal illness or a genetic disorder, the risk is somewhat higher. However, on average, if an intrauterine foetal death or stillbirth occurs, then your partner's chance of a successful future pregnancy is over 90 per cent.

Trawling the message boards on the Internet, it became apparent that, as well as having to experience still- birth, mothers were equally devastated when, soon after, their milk came in. Many reported that as a form of catharsis they would, or even had to, express this milk to relieve the physical and emotional ache. It is actually possible to donate breast milk specifically for the benefit of premature babies. If this is a route your partner wishes to take it is important to check that your local hospital has a milk bank. There are support organizations available; some of them are listed in Chapter 12.

The Emotional Effects

The emotional effect on the couple when things go wrong will depend, like most things, on the temperaments of the individuals involved. In my own case, I became progressively worse at dealing with the miscarriages each time one occurred.

Whether you feel 'a bit upset' or 'devastated' is your own issue and shouldn't open you up for criticism from anyone else. People deal with grief and loss in their own way and there is no right or wrong way to react. Some might find solace in work, or a couple of pints at the pub, or a chance for some uninterrupted thinking and an opportunity to reflect. Many find that they just want to be able to talk to their partners about it, and their partners need to talk to them. It is not uncommon to feel alone and isolated, and that is where your partner can support you. You may find, if you needed reminding, that as well as being a lover and a partner you have in her a best friend who has just been through the same experience.

Most fathers I spoke to who had been through some of the situations listed above reported feeling a huge sense of loss, especially those that lost their unborn child. Grief is a natural reaction and should be accepted if not embraced; you will both take time to heal.

Whatever problems might complicate your partner's pregnancy or the birth of your child, you will be the one person that can help make the decisions and provide the support. Good luck with whatever decisions the two of you make.

12. Learning the Lingo

weird
cravings

Pregnancy comes with its own sub-language and the sooner you learn the lingo, the better. Most of the words hardly run off the tongue (unless you were schooled in Latin and Greek), but to avoid looking like an eejit – a buffoon who doesn't know his pethidine from his cocaine – it's best to try to familiarize yourself with some of them from the outset. So, in some kind of semi-chronological order, here they are:

The Pregnancy:

PREGNANT [a; preg-nant] – heavy with child, the easiest of them all
UTERUS [n; yewt-errr-us] – also known as womb; highly complex baby-growing apparatus containing your baby
ANTENATAL [v; anti-nay-tal] sometimes called PRE-NATAL – the period before your baby is born; literally, before birth

POSTNATAL [v; u-can-open-your-eyes-now] – all is well, pregnancy is over

TRIMESTERS [n; try-messed-hers] – three distinct periods of pregnancy, each lasting approximately three months. The first and third are the worst, the second is not too bad at all (at least for you)

MORNING SICKESS [n; puke-lots-loudly] – intense nausea caused by hormones such as PROGESTERONE and OESTROGEN (see below), suffered throughout the day, usually in the early stages of pregnancy, although it can last for months PROGESTERONE [n; pro-jest-err-own] and OESTROGEN [n; east-row-jen] – differing levels of hormones in your partner's body which play absolute havoc with her mood, appetite and general behaviour; very useful for baby's development PILES [n; sore-bum] – little grape-like areas on or around her anus, which your partner may suffer from during pregnancy, and which really hurt

BABY ACCESSORIES [n; expensive-stuff-you-won't-use] – including, but not limited to, a pushchair, sterilizer, breast- pump, clothes, cot, car seat and baby gym

COLOSTRUM [n; coll-ost-strum] – the stuff that makes your partner's breasts magically double in size; in effect it is pre- milk and will be your baby's first meal

The Birth:

LABOUR [n; no-one-told-me-it-would-be-as-bad-as-this] – the end of pregnancy, the process of giving birth BRAXTON HICKS CONTRACTIONS [n; Brax-ton-hix-con-trac- shons] – sometimes mistaken for labour, these are warm-up exercises for the uterus so that it can get ready to push properly

BROKEN WATERS [n; bro-ken war-terz] – when the bag of fluid surrounding and protecting your baby in the uterus ruptures – inevitably happens while shopping in Sainsbury's or at some other inconvenient and embarrassing time

INDUCED LABOUR [n; in-juiced lay-bor] – like jump-starting your car, the labour is brought on through natural or medical methods

CONTRACTIONS [n; con-cen-trate-on-your-breathing] – the uterus reshaping itself to force a very large baby out of a very small hole

DILATED CERVIX [n; dial-8-ed ser-vicks] – when the cervix (part of your partner's uterus) has opened widely enough to allow baby's exit from the womb

MIDWIFE [n; mid-to-large armed women] – she is your best friend for as long as you are in that hospital. Her word is law and she knows what she is doing

ANAESTHETIST [n; person-with-long-needle] – person who administers pain relief during labour. Don't be alarmed if their hand shakes; it seems to be part of the job requirement EPIDURAL [n; hard-core-injection-into-your-partner's-back] – injection that will numb most of the pain of our partners contractions, but may impede her ability to push

TENS MACHINE [n; tenz ma-sheen] – ridiculous pads placed on your partner's back that send electrical impulses, on demand. Allegedly used for pain relief in labour PETHIDINE [n; peth-a-deen] – morphine-like drug that makes your partner forget about childbirth and recount Janis Joplin lyrics

ENTONOX [n; gas-and-air] – laughing gas; not enough to numb a tooth extraction and certainly not enough to make childbirth much more bearable

EPISIOTOMY [n; ep-izzy-ottomi] – a deft slice of the scalpel that opens that particularly sensitive piece of flesh between the opening of the vagina and the anus to help the birth progress

CAESAREAN SECTION [n; slice-open-pull-cry] – the medical procedure that is employed when a vaginal birth is not possible; a small incision is made and within minutes, if not seconds, a baby is brought into the world

PLACENTA [n; it's-not-over-yet] – your baby's life-support system during pregnancy. Sometimes referred to as the afterbirth, it's a purple mess that will be passed, or removed in the case of caesarean sections, shortly after your baby is born. It's not pretty, but you really will have seen it all by this stage.

Which Leads Us Finally To:

BIRTH [n; missed-it-because-I-passed-out] – the meaning of life, your role and purpose; a very messy affair that will leave lasting memories for the rest of your life

FATHER [n; happiest-man-on-planet] – the weight of responsibility will hit you like a bat across the head, but you'll be ready, and what's more you'll love it.

13. Useful Contacts

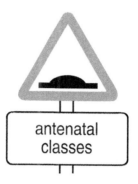

There are both good and bad sources of information available on the Internet, in the telephone directory, and advertised on bad photocopies for 20p a week in the local newsagents. The Internet especially is a constantly changing phenomenon and therefore good (and bad) sites are forever popping up and dropping off. There follows a list of what in my opinion, are useful websites, telephone numbers and addresses that relate to specific chapters in this book. All links were checked at the time of going to press. I cannot vouch for the medical accuracy of the data contained in websites, as a few of them might have been created by people with too much time on their hands, who may have experienced pregnancy and birth only once (a bit like me really!)

I have grouped them geographically to try to make everything as helpful as possible.

United Kingdom

Pregnancy - (General)
www.mothersbliss.co.uk
www.babycentre.com
www.parentlineplus.org.uk
(0800 800 2222)

Family Planning Association
www.fpa.org.uk

Relationships
http://www.relate.org.uk/

Stillbirth
Further advice about registering a stillbirth in England or Wales may be
obtained from your local registrar or from:

General Register Office
Room D209, Smedley Hydro, Trafalgar Road
Southport, Merseyside, PR8 2HH Telephone:
+44 (0)151 471 4805
www.uk-sands.org

Miscarriage www.miscarriageassociation.org.uk

Action For Sick Children
0800 074 4519

Down's Syndrome Association
020 8682 4001

Antenatal Results And Choices (ARC)
020 76310285

Midwives
Independent Midwives Association
0208 406 3172

Water Birth Hire Active Birth Centre
0207 482 5554

TENS Hire
www.mothersbliss.co.uk/nine/labour/tenshire.asp
www.abbytenshire.co.uk/

Postnatal Depression
MAMA (meet a mum association)
0208 768 0123
Association Of Postnatal Illness
0207 386 0868

The Samaritans
The Samaritans offer help and advice on most subjects, although they weren't too keen to come round when we asked for some assistance with repainting a bedroom, but there you go.
Tel: +353 1 671 0071
www.samaritans.org.uk
E: jo@samaritans.org.uk

Wills
www.willdrafters.com
www.searchwill.co.uk
www.easierwills.co.uk

Republic of Ireland

Pregnancy
www.eumom.com
www.baby-parenting.com

The Samaritans 0330 094 5717

United States of America

Miscarriage

www.babycenter.com/refcap/4006.html

Pregnancy
http://pregnancy.about.com/
www.pregnancytoday.com/
www.childbirth.org
www.fitpregnancy.com

TENS Hire
www.tensproducts.com

Australia and New Zealand

Pregnancy
http://australia.babyzone.com
www.huggies.com/au/
www.ninemonths.com.au

Miscarriage
www.miscarriage.org.nz/

Websites of Interest:

www.jonsmith.net
www.balkonfilms.com

Afterword

No guide is ever definitive, but I hope that *The Bloke's Guide to Pregnancy* has helped you to understand some of the changes in you, your partner and your lives. A birth is a beautiful thing, and when you look upon your new-born child for the first time, for that split second, everything makes sense. There will never be a book written that will definitively capture your own personal experience week by week, but I hope that, you can relate to at least some of the aspects I have explored. Luckily, pregnancy and birth are, despite their frequency, still very much a unique experience for the individual mother and father; it is important to enjoy and appreciate the whole experience.

Your partner's pregnancy can be harrowing and stressful. It can also be a lot of fun, believe it or not, and if nothing else, for all the stretching it might do to your relationship, paradoxically it will also help it to bind – making you an even stronger unit.

When the engorged breasts are long gone; when the 3 a.m. visits to the loo are a distant memory, and when your child begins walking, talking and even answering you back, in a cheeky 'butter wouldn't melt' way, you might fleetingly wish you could turn back the clock to your young, free and childless days; but deep down, once you become a father, even for the second, third or fourth time, you wouldn't have it any other way. I promise.

To all the new dads (in waiting) out there:

Congratulations.

Jon Smith, Liverpool, England

Acknowledgements

Without the birth of my daughter Alia, I would not be the person I am today, nor would I have had reason to write this book. Alia is, and will continue to be, a huge inspiration to me. I hope she grows to realize that her existence, even *in utero*, has made a massive and positive difference to my life.

A huge thank you to my ex-wife, Lisa, for her part in my journey into fatherhood – and for allowing me to share many real life (and very embarrassing) anecdotes throughout the book. To my parents Pat and Hugh, for proving that good parents can love even the most rebellious of offspring.

This book would not have been possible without the detailed, sometimes harrowing, often funny, and incredibly insightful testimonies of the 117 fathers interviewed in Toytopia between July and December 2002. Thank you especially to Zazz, Malcolm, Chris Hitchcock and Kevin McKidd.

Grateful thanks also to the original publisher of this book, Michelle Pilley, and all the team at Hay House UK, for being patient and professional enough, to help grow my manuscript from a disjointed collection of ideas into a good book. Thanks also to my editor, Louise McNamara – I'm glad one of us knows our past participle from our elbow.

And finally, a thank you to you, the reader; by buying this book you prove that there is an appetite for more male-directed information about pregnancy, also proving that some of us 'blokes' want to be as involved and included throughout the pregnancy as in every other stage of our child's life.

ABOUT THE AUTHOR

Jon Smith, father of four, lives and writes in Liverpool, England. Jon was awarded a BA (Hons) in American Studies from The University of Reading (and The University of Texas at Austin) and a MA in Screenwriting from Bournemouth University. He writes novels, musical theatre, television drama and feature films. He is currently Chief Marketing Officer of Autocab and serves on the board of directors.

Jon is the author of 14 books including *The Bloke's Guide to Pregnancy, The Bloke's 100 Top Tips For Surviving Pregnancy* and *The Bloke's Guide to Babies*.

www.jonsmith.net

Other Titles by Jon Smith

The Bloke's Guide to Babies *(Hay House)*

The Bloke's 100 top tips to surviving pregnancy *(Hay House)*

The Bloke's Guide to baby gadgets *(Hay House)*

The Bloke's Guide to getting hitched *(Hay House)*

Toytopia *(Wrecking Ball Press)*

Be* #1 on *Google *(McGraw Hill)*

Get into bed with Google *(Infinite Ideas)*

Grow Your Business with Google Adwords *(McGraw Hill)*

Dominate Your Market with Twitter *(Infinite Ideas)*

Web Sites that Work *(Infinite Ideas)*

Smarter Business Start-Ups *(Infinite Ideas)*

Start an Online Business *(In Easy Steps)*

Digital Marketing for Businesses *(In Easy Steps)*

Related titles by Jon Smith

BALKON
media